D1615426

JEWISH MUSEUM BERLIN

HEINRICH V. KLEIST (1810-1811)

E.T.A. HOFFMANN CHARLOTTENSTR. 56

RACHEL WARNHAGEN FRANZÖSISCHE STR. 20

HEINRICH HEINE MOHRENSTR. 32

MIES VAN DER ROHE

MEMORIAL 24 AM KARLSBAD

RACHEL VARNHAGEN (1771-1833)

(1791-1834)

JEWISH MUSEUM BERLIN

Architect Daniel Libeskind
with a photo essay by Hélène Binet

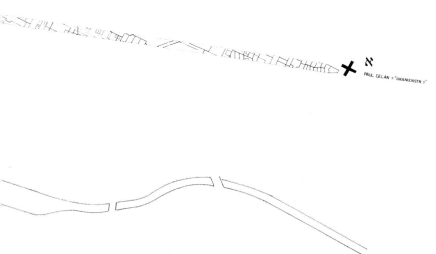

PAUL CELAN = 'ORANIENSTR 1'

G+B Arts International 1999

Contents

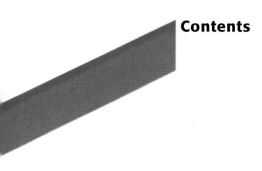

ISBN 90-5701-252-9

Design: Sonja Hennersdorf & Martina Sailer, Berlin
Principal Type: Formata
Printed on Biomatt
Production: Ruksaldruck, Germany

Only rarely does one have the opportunity to direct an institution that is history-making both for its work and for its building. I am fortunate to have such an opportunity in the creation of the new Berlin Jewish Museum within one of the world's most notable structures. Daniel Libeskind's extraordinary architecture challenges everyone – museum visitor and museum worker alike – to rethink the role of the museum in society. Rich in symbolism, the museum's design integrates concepts related to the tragic Jewish past with a future-oriented aesthetic asserting the vitality of Jewish life.

The combination of past, present, and future has also determined the museum's program, which aims to extend public understanding of the complex Jewish presence in Germany over many centuries. I am grateful to Daniel Libeskind for having assured us of a museum that now takes its place among the world's celebrated buildings. My personal commitment is to use this challenging, imaginative, and groundbreaking architectural presence as a means for creating an equally distinguished new Jewish Museum Berlin.

W. Michael Blumenthal

Three basic ideas formed the foundation for the Jewish Museum design: first, the impossibility of understanding the history of Berlin without understanding the enormous intellectual, economic, and cultural contribution made by its Jewish citizens; second the necessity to integrate the meaning of the Holocaust, both physically and spiritually, into the consciousness and memory of the city of Berlin; third, that only through acknowledging and incorporating this erasure and void of Berlinís Jewish life can the history of Berlin and Europe have a human future.   D. L.

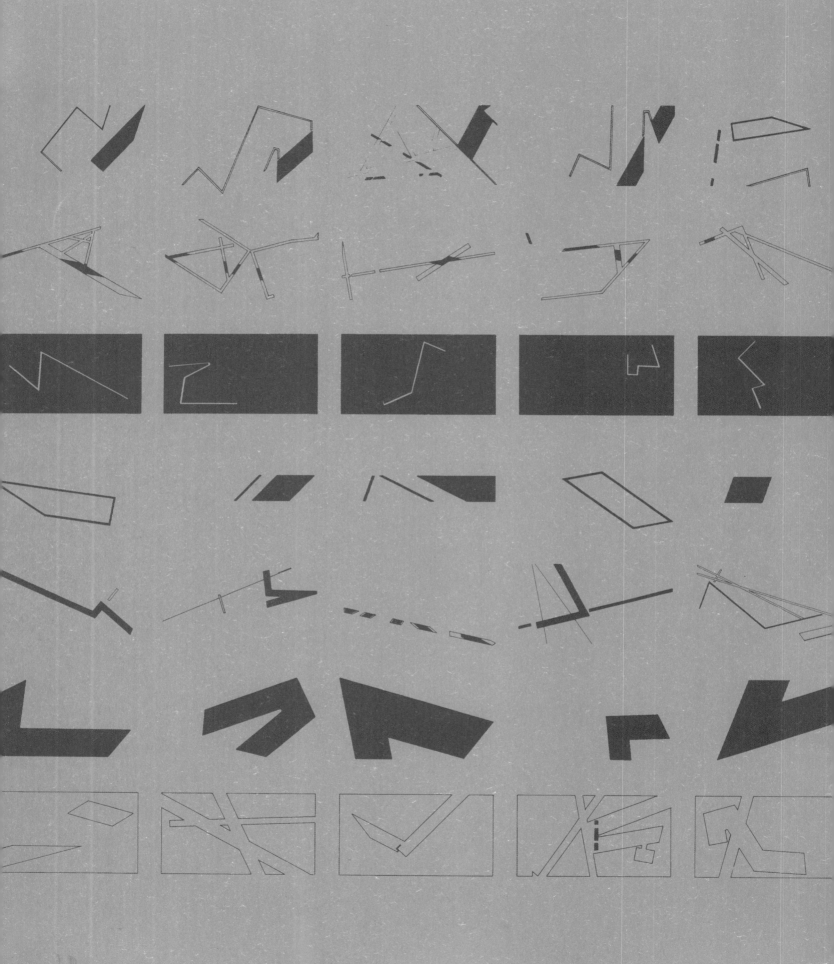

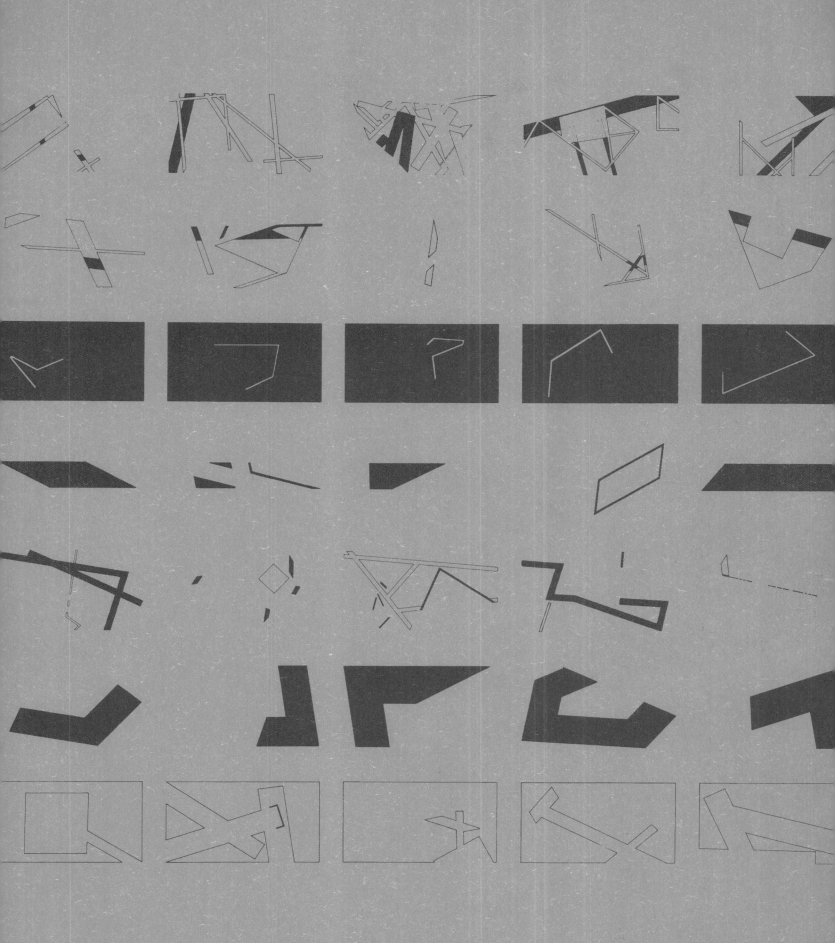

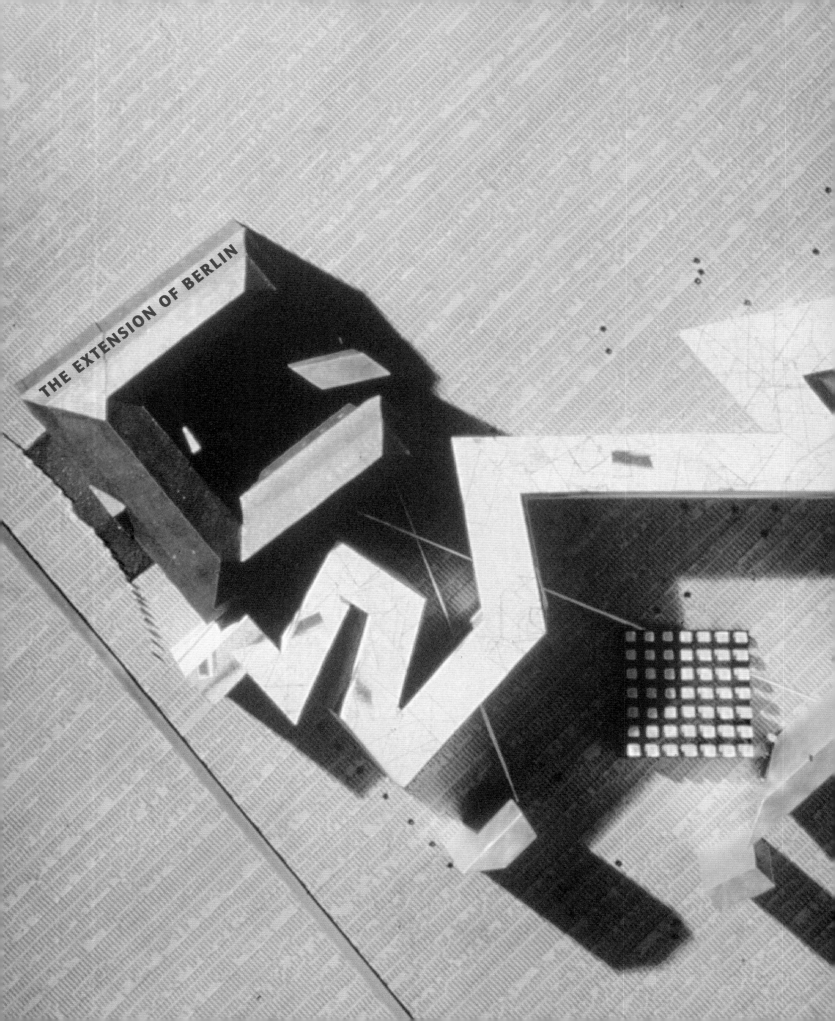

THE EXTENSION OF BERLIN

Daniel Libeskind talks with Doris Erbacher and Peter Paul Kubitz

Doris Erbacher and Peter Paul Kubitz: The Jewish Museum is located near both the center of Berlin and the ruins of the once existing Anhalter Bahnhof Station. Did the images of a demolished Berlin shape the design of your museum? Was your impression of Berlin in 1945 a premise for your work? Are these images, perhaps, part of the creative basis upon which you build?

Daniel Libeskind: It is not a basis, but it is certainly true that the destruction of Berlin was the greatest event in the history of the city: It completely changed the face of Berlin and what it is. Consequently, anybody working in Berlin would inevitably have to deal with what to do after such an incredible devastation, as well as determine what that history means for tomorrow.

But it is really more a question of how one deals with ruins and with history: Does one wipe them out? Does one simply forget about them? Or does one deal with them in a constructive way, as they are part of the memory of the city?

The Jewish Museum stands in a sort of kaleidoscopic area which is the product of many different histories of Berlin. Surrounding the Museum is an 18th-century Baroque building, some 19th-century fragments, the Mendelsohn building from the 1920s, the housing blocks from the 60s, the IBA projects from the 70s, and a newly built flower market. This diversity illustrates the multiple and plural history of Berlin.

These buildings from the 60s and 70s are basically traces of the destruction of Berlin. After all, the site on which you are building the "Erweiterungsbau," the Jewish Museum, is quite a heterogeneous one.

The different strands of memories and of both urban and architectural forms should be woven into the integrity of the city. The city is a rich thing. It is not something made out of one-dimensional ideas, but rather it is a product developed from many imaginations, many people, and many histories.

I am not interested in simply forgetting the complexity of a city and treating it as if it were a *tabula rasa*. I want to be aware of Berlin's various undercurrents, which carry with them the flotsam and jetsam of human discourse.

Certainly Berlin is no *tabula rasa*, but differs significantly from other cities.

Of course, it is different from other cities, and I think that is the unique quality that is here. Both the memory and the history of the city are so substantial that even visitors who hardly know Berlin of the 1920s or 1890s attempt to see through the vacancy of the sites to understand what that history might have looked like.

I think that is the singular quality of Berlin. It is a city which is enigmatic. It has a charisma: the name itself stands for so many different things. Moreover, it continues to have that function even though its spaces might have changed beyond current memory.

Berlin is more interesting to me than any city. I came here for a very specific reason: to build the Jewish Museum. Berlin, as the center of the destruction of European Jews, was the center of both devastation and transformation. The modern world is inseparable from the name Berlin.

view from Lindenstraße

Considering that you see Berlin in this light, could you explain how you combine the political and the aesthetic aspects of architecture?

Architecture is part of the politeia. It is a political act; it is not a private one. It is not just sitting in a studio and inventing whatever one wants to invent. It is a deeply political act, as it can only be built through agreement, through discussion, through discourse, and through a democratic view of what is best for the citizens of a city.

One has to remember that the city is not only built out of stone, glass, and concrete. It is built out of its inhabitants – the citizens who are really the substance of the city, not simply the walls and spaces of the city. So, of course, when considering the political dimension of architecture, one should keep in mind that architecture represents every wall, every window, and every space that has to do with an individual's visual perspective, memory, imagination, and dreams.

Would you say the same for private architecture, for an architect who builds private buildings?

No. A private building is different, although it lives in the city. For better or for worse, I have never been commissioned to erect a private building. However, in Greek the word 'private' is 'idiota.' 'Idiota' is used to differentiate between the private and the public members of society. And, of course, private houses are to some degree a destruction of the city itself. The privatization of a city's land and treating that land, as if it were a private place, destroys the urban spirit of great cities as we have known them throughout history.

the "Names" model

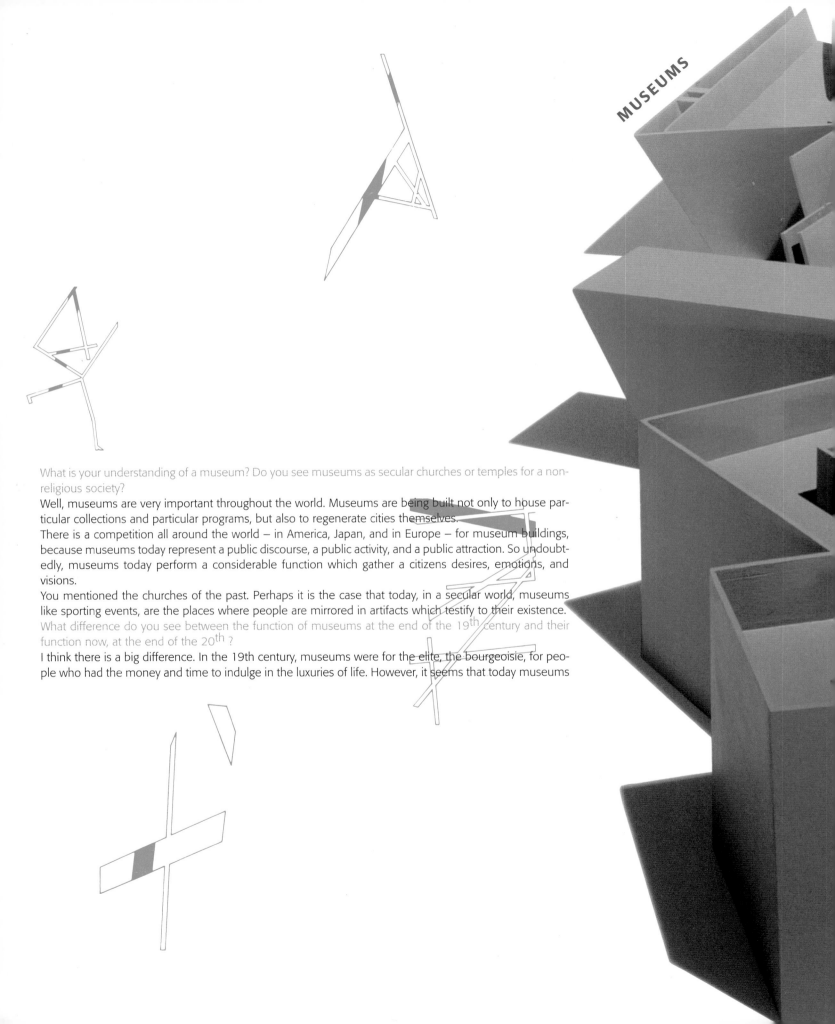

What is your understanding of a museum? Do you see museums as secular churches or temples for a non-religious society?

Well, museums are very important throughout the world. Museums are being built not only to house particular collections and particular programs, but also to regenerate cities themselves.

There is a competition all around the world – in America, Japan, and in Europe – for museum buildings, because museums today represent a public discourse, a public activity, and a public attraction. So undoubtedly, museums today perform a considerable function which gather a citizens desires, emotions, and visions.

You mentioned the churches of the past. Perhaps it is the case that today, in a secular world, museums like sporting events, are the places where people are mirrored in artifacts which testify to their existence.

What difference do you see between the function of museums at the end of the 19th century and their function now, at the end of the 20th ?

I think there is a big difference. In the 19th century, museums were for the elite, the bourgeoisie, for people who had the money and time to indulge in the luxuries of life. However, it seems that today museums

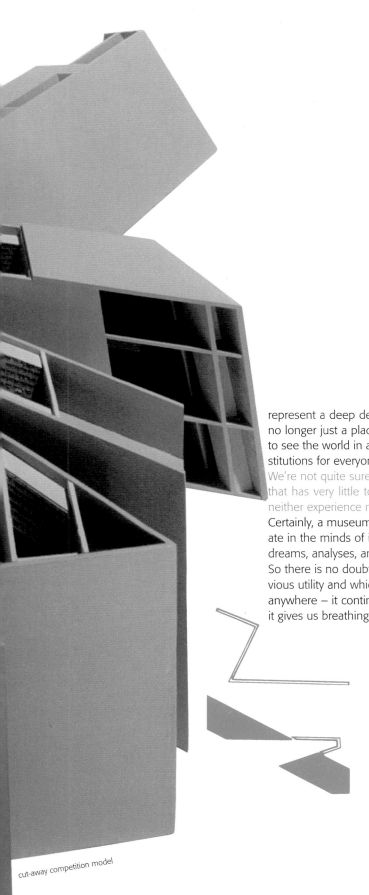

represent a deep desire for public participation. Everyone has the right to visit a museum. A museum is no longer just a place to dream; instead, it is a place to be educated, a place to be given new skills, and to see the world in a new way. Accordingly, museums are no longer simply elitist institutions. They are institutions for everyone, and they play a large role in shaping the evolving view of a city.

We're not quite sure we can agree with you. Don't you think there is a lot of hype going on in museums that has very little to do with education, an event culture that allows neither meditation, nor reflection, neither experience nor speculation in the positive sense of the word?

Certainly, a museum works on many different levels. But if a museum is good, then it continues to operate in the minds of its visitors after its closing hours. It continues to be an image which can be filled with dreams, analyses, and thoughts.

So there is no doubt that a museum performs many other functions, which stretch beyond the most obvious utility and which can be discussed in very objective terms. But that is also true of good architecture anywhere – it continues to be something that does not simply haunt us in a negative sense, but instead it gives us breathing room to speculate and to think of new ways of being.

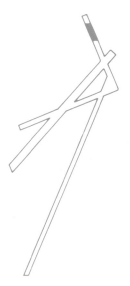

cut-away competition model

above: spatial situation of the museum,
collage and colorprint 1990

left: acustic and optical issues,
collage and colorprint 1990

below: urban issue,
collage and colorprint 1990

'Erweiterungsbau' – that is a very interesting word, because 'Erweiterungsbau' means extension. The extension of both Berlin's history and Jewish history is not merely the extension of a building form, rather it is the extension of both the program and the idea of extending Jewish heritage across the abyss created by the destruction of European Jewry.

The 'Erweiterung' poses more problems than simply building a bridge out of concrete or glass and connecting a Baroque building to a new building. It represents a philosophical and a cultural reality that reaches beyond simply constructing walls, touching the existential core of "extension." Ultimately architecture is based on very pedestrian and prosaic things: building foundations, erecting buildings, and making spaces for particular functions. But, I think, in a global sense, the 'Erweiterungsbau' stands for much more than simply creating more space and more square meters. It stands for a new relationship between the old history, the Baroque history, and the depth of that history in contemporary Berlin; a new relationship to a history that can hardly be matched and pieced together into a whole.

Without this vision, it would be impossible to combine the incredible legacy of Baroque Berlin – with its Jews, its Enlightenment, its extraordinary ideas of modernity, and its ideas that have undoubtedly changed the world – and the vacuity which is also connected to this history. So this is the contradictory, challenging, and very exciting story to present to the public.

Please explain the relationship between the Baroque building and what is called the "Erweiterungsbau" in German.

Blum, Frieda, geb.   Bloch, A...   Birnbaum, Henri   Bickel, Frieda   Bernhard, Max
Blum, Friedrich   Bloch, Anna   Birnbaum, Herta   Bickel, Melli, geb   Bernhard, Max
Blum, Georg   Bloch, Antonie   Birnbaum, Herta   Bickel, Siegmund   Bernhard, Max
Blum, Gertrud   Bloch, Armin   Birnbaum, Ida, g   Bickert, Bertha,   Bernhard, Meta,
Blum, Gustav   Bloch, Arthur   Birnbaum, Herta   Bickhardt, Betty,   Bernhard, Oscar
Blum, Gustav   Bloch, Artur   Birnbaum, Josef   Bickhardt, Edgar   Bernhard, Paul
Blum, Gustav   Bloch, Auguste, g   Birnbaum, Josef   Bickhardt, Edith   Bernhard, Paula,
Blum, Hedwig   Bloch, Babette, g   Birnbaum, Juliau   Bickhardt, Gertru   Bernhard, Richar
Blum, Hedwig, ge   Bloch, Bernhard   Birnbaum, Julius   Bickhardt, Jakob   Bernhard, Ruth
Blum, Hedwig, ge   Bloch, Berta   Birnbaum, Julius   Bickhardt, Jakob   Bernhard, Sara
Blum, Hedwig, ge   Bloch, Berta, geb   Birnbaum, Julius   Bickhardt, Kaeth   Bernhard, Siegfr
Blum, Helene   Bloch, Berta, geb   Birnbaum, Klara,   Bickhardt, Thekl   Bernhard, Siegfr
Blum, Helene, ge   Bloch, Berta M.   Birnbaum, Kurt   Bickhardt, Theres   Bernhard, Susan
Blum, Henriette,   Bloch, Bertha, ge   Birnbaum, Lea, g   Bicz, Samuel   Bernhard, Ursula
Blum, Henry   Bloch, Bertha, ge   Birnbaum, Lina   Biczunsky, Leopo   Bernhard, Wilhe
Blum, Henry   Bloch, Berthold   Birnbaum, Marth   Biczunsky, Marga   Bernhard, Willy
Blum, Herman   Bloch, Betty, geb   Birnbaum, Marth   Bie-Milchner, An   Bernhardt, Amal
Blum, Hermine, g   Bloch, Bonna   Birnbaum, Maryl   Bieber, Alfred   Bernhardt, Anna,
Blum, Hildegard   Bloch, Bonna, geb   Birnbaum, Mathi   Bieber, Alfred   Bernhardt, Berta
Blum, Hugo   Bloch, Bruno   Birnbaum, Max   Bieber, Annette D   Bernhardt, Fanny
Blum, Hugo   Bloch, Camilla   Birnbaum, Meilic   Bieber, Arthur   Bernhardt, Guent
Blum, Ida, geb. C   Bloch, Camilla   Birnbaum, Morit   Bieber, Brigitte, g   Bernhardt, Hans
Blum, Ida, geb. C   Bloch, Caroline   Birnbaum, Pessel   Bieber, Denny   Bernhardt, Hans
Blum, Ida, geb. H   Bloch, Chana   Birnbaum, Rafae   Bieber, Erich   Bernhardt, Hedw
Blum, Ida, geb. L   Bloch, Chana, ge   Birnbaum, Ruche   Bieber, Fanny   Bernhardt, Herta
Blum, Ida, geb. R   Bieber, Florentin   Bernhardt, Hugo,
                Bieber, Frieda   Bernhardt, Ingeb
                Bieber, Friedrich   Bernhardt, Kurt

What is your relationship to E.T.A. Hoffmann, what is your affinity to him, what are your associations regarding him and how does that related to the Jewish Museum?

I imagine that many people have read E. T. A Hoffmann at some point in their lives. I have always loved E. T. A Hoffmann, and I was stunned when I started working on the Museum to discover that he was a lawyer in the *Altbau*, in the *Kollegienhaus*, and that he lived just a few blocks north of the Museum. As I began designing the building, I thought of specific people who had lived in Berlin. Abstract notions of space, time, and life did not interest me as much as actual people did. In addition to considering E. T. A. Hoffmann, I thought of all of the hundreds of thousands of Berliners who are no longer here to speak on behalf of the new Berlin. These people constitute the *Berliner Luft* – the air across Berlin which mixes with the air of history to shape the city. For those who are aware of it, it is extremely palpable; however, for those who are unaware of it, the air is there nevertheless.

Berlin's history is like a kaleidoscope; it's crazy, and yet there is a kind of logic inherent to it. If you go through the city with open eyes, if you can sense this echo of history, then you realize that the secrets of history continue to be present.

detail of model 'Garden of Exile'

center: study model 'Garden of Exile'

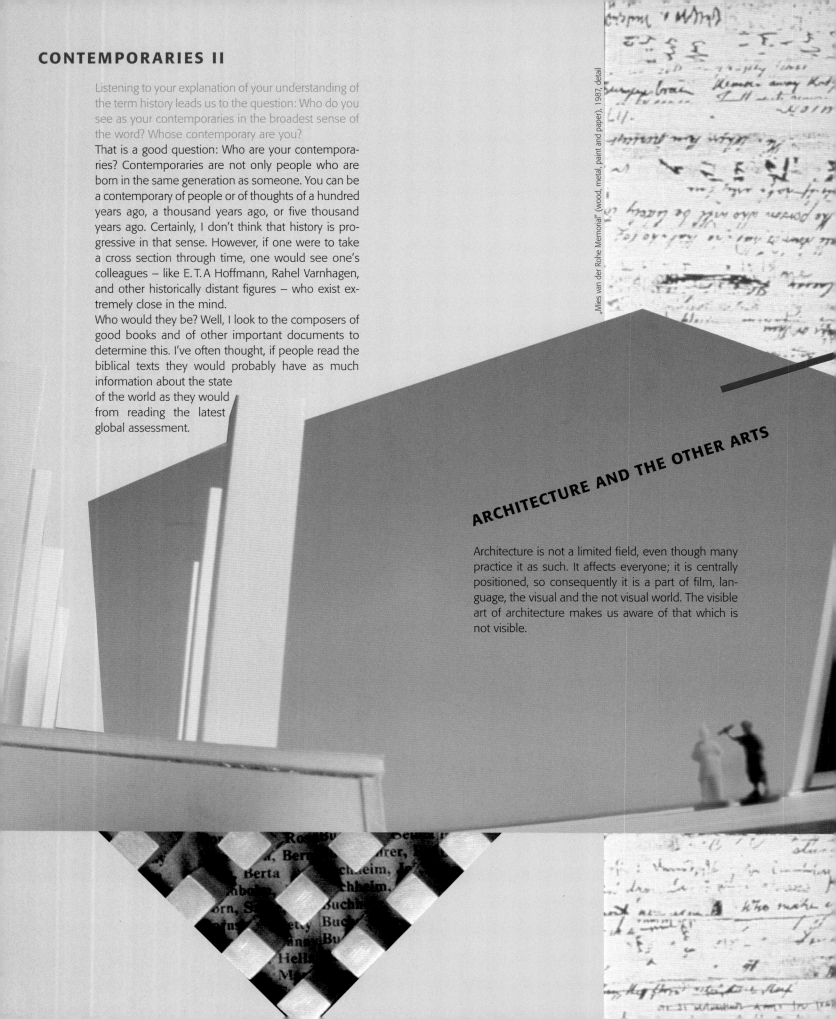

CONTEMPORARIES II

Listening to your explanation of your understanding of the term history leads us to the question: Who do you see as your contemporaries in the broadest sense of the word? Whose contemporary are you?

That is a good question: Who are your contemporaries? Contemporaries are not only people who are born in the same generation as someone. You can be a contemporary of people or of thoughts of a hundred years ago, a thousand years ago, or five thousand years ago. Certainly, I don't think that history is progressive in that sense. However, if one were to take a cross section through time, one would see one's colleagues – like E.T.A Hoffmann, Rahel Varnhagen, and other historically distant figures – who exist extremely close in the mind.

Who would they be? Well, I look to the composers of good books and of other important documents to determine this. I've often thought, if people read the biblical texts they would probably have as much information about the state of the world as they would from reading the latest global assessment.

ARCHITECTURE AND THE OTHER ARTS

Architecture is not a limited field, even though many practice it as such. It affects everyone; it is centrally positioned, so consequently it is a part of film, language, the visual and the not visual world. The visible art of architecture makes us aware of that which is not visible.

„Mies van der Rohe Memorial" (wood, metal, paint and paper), 1987, detail

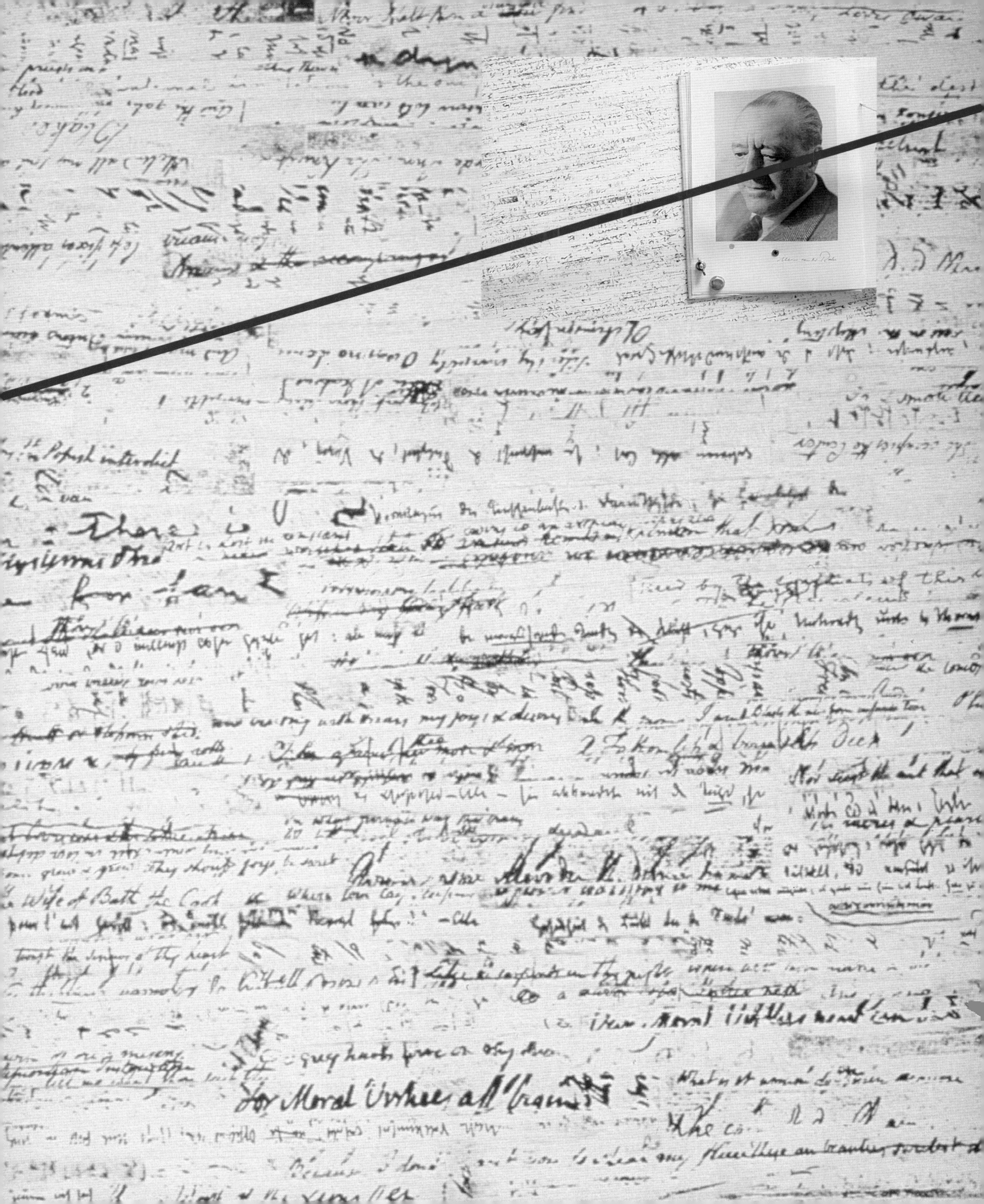
Wife of Bath

The Jewish Museum has been provided with topographical signs and biographical references which together form a matrix...

I used many devices to structure the Museum. I did not merely try to fit the building into its urban environment. Nor did I simply try to make spaces and mold them to their functions. Instead, I attempted to extend the building towards the traces of the unborn. The city's orientation is no longer so obvious because of the changes wrought by the destruction of Berlin starting in 1933 and ending after this cataclysm.

So yes, I did build the Museum on the basis of addressing points, for example, of connections between Berliners and Jews who lived around Lindenstrasse. Addresses which are now hardly visible because the city has changed around them.

In the structure of the building, I sought to embody the matrix of connections which might seem irrational today but are, nevertheless, visible and rationalized by relationships between people. I attempted to represent the names and numbers associated with the Jewish Berliners, with the 200,000 Jews who are no longer here to constitute that fabric of Berlin which was so successful in business and the arts, intellectual, professional, and cultural fields.

And I used para-architectural means to achieve those organisations. For example, I used Walter Benjamin's text, *Einbahnstrasse*, neither as a metaphor nor as an inspiration to build a building, but rather to make a building whose use would open up that uni-directional text to other perspectives. There are sixty stations, stop-gaps along the distorted Star of David, which in the text, as well as in the building of the Jewish Museum, tracing apocalyptic Berlin.

I also delved into Arnold Schoenberg's unfinished opera *Moses und Aron* in a very pragmatic way for the spacing of the music's soundlessness after the break in the second act. This spacing cannot be continued in any musical form, but it can exist, in the space of the void of architecture. These are the devices and the thoughts which organized that geometry.

Could you please elaborate on the importance of Schoenberg's opera *Moses and Aron*, and especially on the significance of the break.

MOSES UND ARON

score of Schoenberg's opera "Moses and Aron"

As you know, Schoenberg, Arnold Schoenberg, and later Aaron Schoenberg, was an assimilated Jew who worked as a professor of music here close to the Berlin Museum. And as times changed, he was made aware of the fact that he was not wanted in the city; finally, he was exiled from Berlin. He had no choice but to leave, although he was the most famous composer, and, in my opinion, one of the great minds of the 20th century.

Moses and Aron was written at this time and around this space. It is not coincidental that the sound came to him right here in Kreuzberg and in Berlin-Mitte. His music is emblematic in every way of what happens to the sound – the conversation between Moses and Aron – which is broken off. Aron speaks on behalf of the people; he is the master of the people's truths; he wants simple and clear answers. Moses, on the otherhand, is hardly able to endure the absence of the Word.

At the end of this break there is the call for the Word. And what is very interesting musically is that there is no more singing in this opera. In a certain way *Moses and Aron* is the last opera. Although operas continued to be written, this opera represents the end. The voice is alone with the orchestra playing one single note – sixty or seventy instruments play one note and then they stop. And the voice calls out; it does not sing; on the contrary, it literally calls out for the Word and for the truth of that absent Word.

I think that this is not only a poignantly unsurpassed

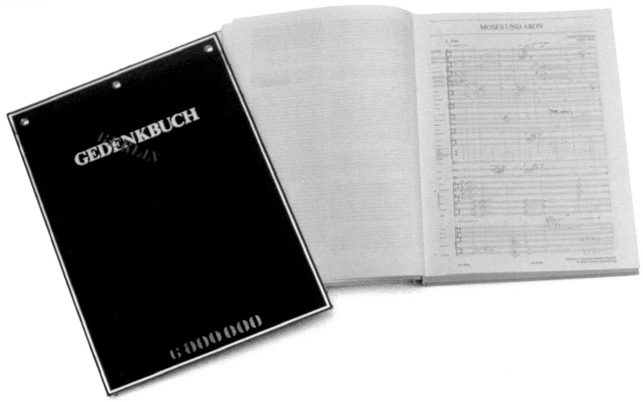

and unsurpassable 20th century musical experience, but it also possesses an architectural dimension. It represents a dimension of the kind of topography which was created by the devastation of humanity.

I think that we are on the pioneering track now in the 20th century – the century in which all of these major events took place. What will happen in the future? What is this world?

Is the break, the silence, the end of Schoenberg's music?

It is actually beyond silence, since silence is always related to sound. It was a definitive break, because although Schoenberg wrote the libretto to the third act, he never put it to music. And I do not think that it was coincidental; it was not because he ran out of ideas, as he continued to write music. Instead, it was because he came to the impasse in which music has no sound-relationship. There is no silence in it either; it contains a kind of continuity which is mysteriously in another dimension of space.

And it is there! It resonates when one listens to it; it resonates when one hears other voices of contemporary music which have picked this aspect out of the microscopic and weak elements of sound and silence. When one looks to the heirs of this music, for example the *Fragmente* of Luigi Nono one sees how it is hardly audible in the reinforced imagination, the imaginary echoes of faith. I believe that these are the issues of contemporary music, as they are the issues of contemporary architecture.

competition text

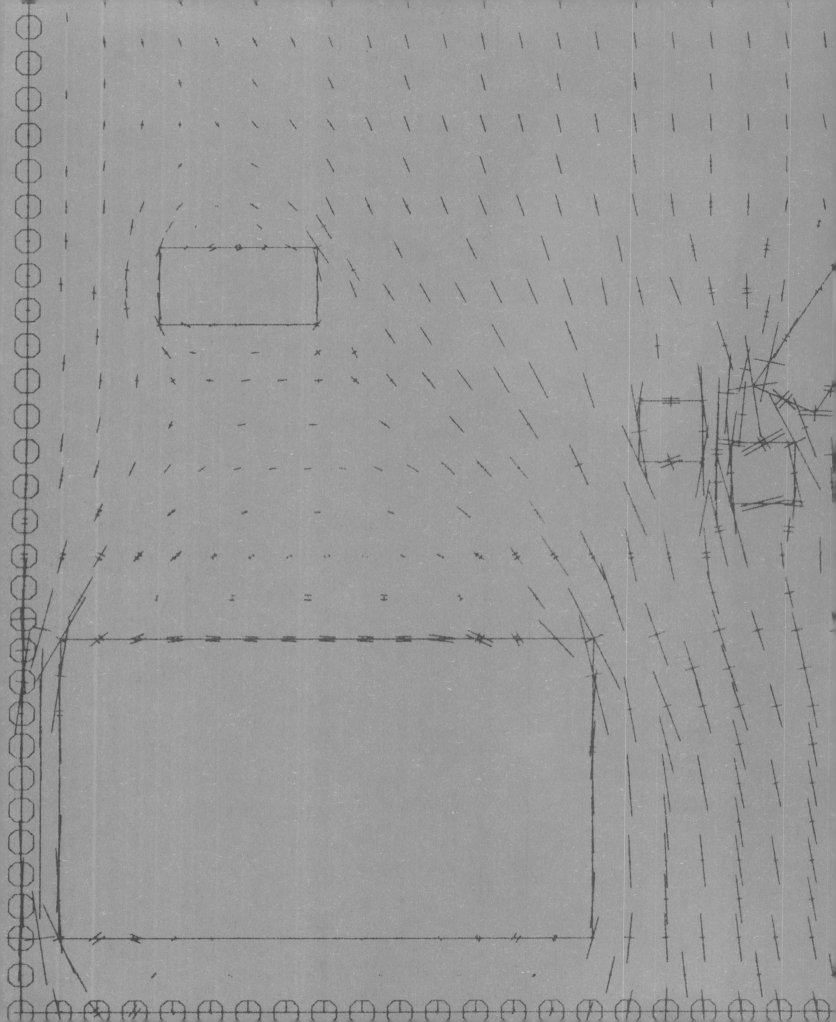

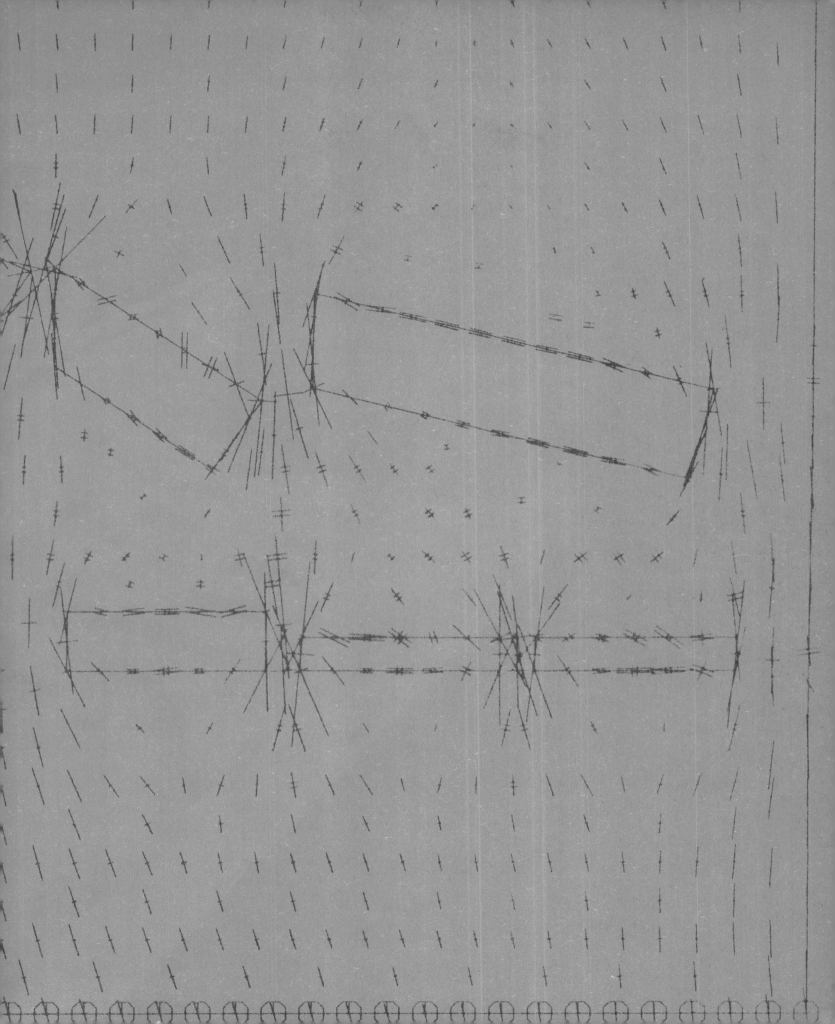

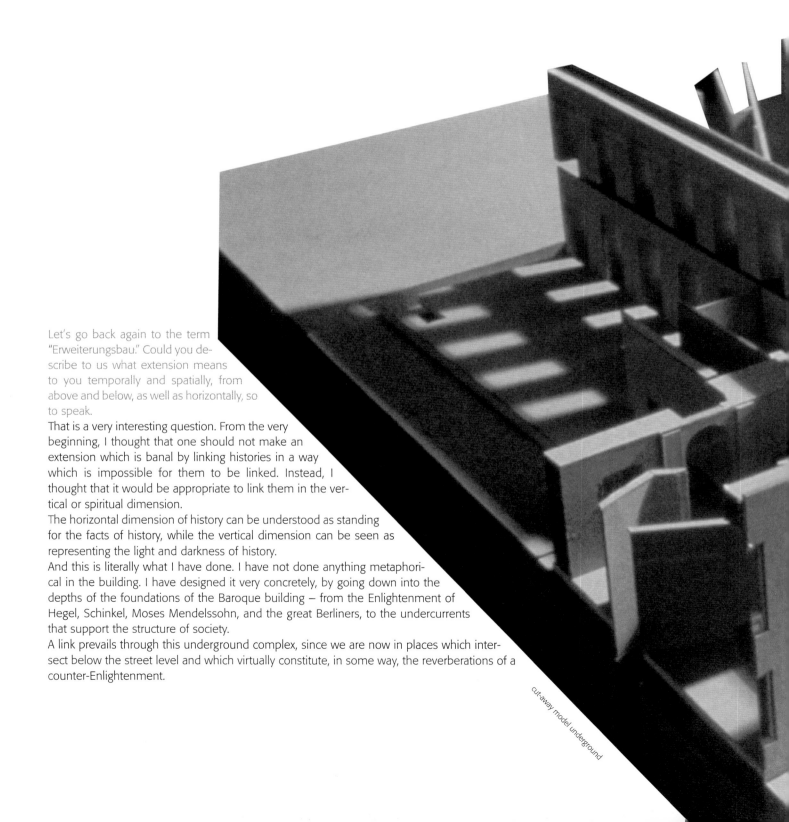

Let's go back again to the term "Erweiterungsbau." Could you de- scribe to us what extension means to you temporally and spatially, from above and below, as well as horizontally, so to speak.

That is a very interesting question. From the very beginning, I thought that one should not make an extension which is banal by linking histories in a way which is impossible for them to be linked. Instead, I thought that it would be appropriate to link them in the ver- tical or spiritual dimension.

The horizontal dimension of history can be understood as standing for the facts of history, while the vertical dimension can be seen as representing the light and darkness of history.

And this is literally what I have done. I have not done anything metaphori- cal in the building. I have designed it very concretely, by going down into the depths of the foundations of the Baroque building – from the Enlightenment of Hegel, Schinkel, Moses Mendelssohn, and the great Berliners, to the undercurrents that support the structure of society.

A link prevails through this underground complex, since we are now in places which inter- sect below the street level and which virtually constitute, in some way, the reverberations of a counter-Enlightenment.

cut-away model underground

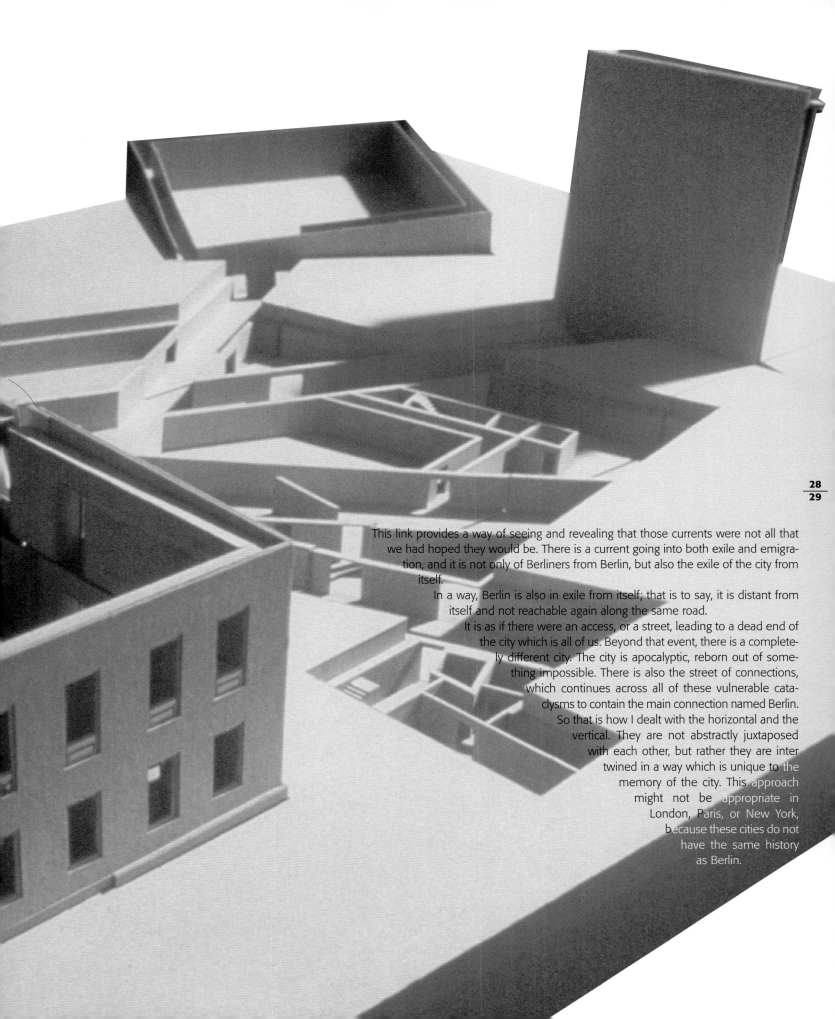

This link provides a way of seeing and revealing that those currents were not all that we had hoped they would be. There is a current going into both exile and emigration, and it is not only of Berliners from Berlin, but also the exile of the city from itself.

In a way, Berlin is also in exile from itself; that is to say, it is distant from itself and not reachable again along the same road.

It is as if there were an access, or a street, leading to a dead end of the city which is all of us. Beyond that event, there is a completely different city. The city is apocalyptic, reborn out of something impossible. There is also the street of connections, which continues across all of these vulnerable cataclysms to contain the main connection named Berlin. So that is how I dealt with the horizontal and the vertical. They are not abstractly juxtaposed with each other, but rather they are intertwined in a way which is unique to the memory of the city. This approach might not be appropriate in London, Paris, or New York, because these cities do not have the same history as Berlin.

"Void" is a concept central to your architecture. How would you translate this term into German?

"Die Leere" is a quality. It is a space you enter in the museum which organizes the museum, and yet it is not part of the museum. It is not heated, it is not air-conditioned, furthermore it is not really a museum space. Yet "Die Leere" is something else – it is the space of Berlin, because it refers to that which can never be exhibited when it comes to the Jewish Berlin history. Humanity reduced to ashes.

So there is nothing except the walls and a line which runs across Berlin. And the line is a white line of light which connects the dream to a tectonic and constructive Berlin of the future. And yet, that one line which is so heterogeneous and so vulnerable, is what I perceive to be the line of Berlin: It is both decisive and mysterious. So "Die Leere" is not some abstract synonym for negativity.

And "Voided Void"?

'Voided Void' means to take that emptiness and to materialize it as a building.

And the 'Voided Void' – the Holocaust Tower, as it is now called – in the Jewish Museum is the space which somehow ends the old history of Berlin. It starts with the pogroms and the anti-Semitic edicts which did not only begin in 1933. They are there in history; they became obvious, irrefutable, and unfortunately irrever-sible in 1933.

From the burning of books and cultural artifacts, the exhibit of which will be shown in the Museum, to the burning of human beings which will be represented by nothing but the names in a *Gedenkbuch** – this is what I mean by the 'voided void'. This bespeaks the nothingness of the nothing.

As a space, the void which cuts through the building is a mirror image of that internal emptiness through the building itself, and which incorporates the sixty stations of Walter Benjamin running across the topography of absence-presence.

In Walter Benjamin's *Thesis on the Philosophy of History* he presents the 'Angel of History.' This angel stares wide-eyed into a past full of catastrophes. At the same time, he is driven by the "force of history," the supposed progress, into an uncertain future.

I am neither a philosopher nor a historian, so I am not really able to comment. Undoubtedly, the 'Angel of History' is a very powerful image. The only angels that I could imagine today are the airplanes that would be able to view the plan of the Museum from above.

Of course, one could obtain a comprehensive impression, like an angel's perspective of the actual shape of the Museum. But I do not think that visitors need to travel in airplanes to obtain this view. They can simply be themselves and enter the world which is very much a part of the traditional Berlin.

The Museum is an unprecedented building. Indeed, it is quite a traditional building. And when one enters it with that awareness, one views it in quite a different light.

There is also the space between the mind and the reality of being a citizen of a place, and the building mirrors this and makes this explicit.

Many see the museum building itself as an exhibit in itself ...

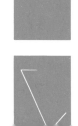

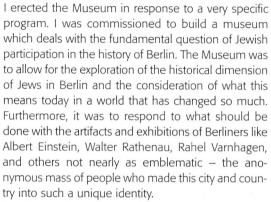

"Architectural Alphabet"

I erected the Museum in response to a very specific program. I was commissioned to build a museum which deals with the fundamental question of Jewish participation in the history of Berlin. The Museum was to allow for the exploration of the historical dimension of Jews in Berlin and the consideration of what this means today in a world that has changed so much. Furthermore, it was to respond to what should be done with the artifacts and exhibitions of Berliners like Albert Einstein, Walter Rathenau, Rahel Varnhagen, and others not nearly as emblematic – the anonymous mass of people who made this city and country into such a unique identity.

I realize that there are people who are skeptical about the relationship between objects and space in the Museum. But people are also skeptical about the history of Berlin. Those very people who never wanted to see that history find it extremely difficult to accept the Museum. They say: 'Mr. Libeskind, now it is very difficult to address this issue.' But yes, it is difficult, and that is why it is so very important to do so.

This is the history, this is the collision, the kaleidoscope of gaps and traces and the intersection of the impossibilities which this building presents to the public through books, artifacts, paintings, sculptures, toys, fashions. This is not a Kaiser's collection, but rather a museum which presents the collections of ordinary citizens. In my opinion, this is what makes the building unique and what makes it a fascinating program to fulfill.

* The Gedenkbuch – Opfer der Verfolgung der Juden was published in two volumes by the Bundesarchiv, Koblenz, and the Internationalen Suchdienst, Avolsen, in 1986.

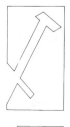

In 1997/1998, eight years after you had won the competition for the building of the Jewish Museum, you took part in a competition for the erection of a central Holocaust Memorial in Berlin. Many intellectuals and artists, not only in Berlin, but throughout Germany, found this superfluous. These critics saw such a memorial already eloquently realized in the Jewish Museum. Thus your proposal for a memorial begs the question: Is there a relationship between your proposal for the Memorial and the design for the Jewish Museum?

The two issues are indeed connected. There is no doubt that the need for a Jewish Museum in the city and the discussion about the need for a memorial are interconnected, as they refer to the same event.

All of your architecture is and shows itself to be conceptual, an architecture of ideas. This is apparent not only in the Jewish Museum, but also in the proposal for the Holocaust Memorial. Could you sketch the ideas behind the memorial for us?

The main reason I took part in the competition for the Memorial is the very fact that people said: "We do not need the Memorial – we already have Libeskind's building." However, the Museum is not a memorial, despite the fact that there are dimensions of memory built into it. The Museum is a museum – it is a space for the encounter of history: a building and not a memorial.

If there is to be a memorial, then I believe it would have to be of a scale and importance that can hold its own against the Brandenburger Tor, the Reichstag (Bundestag) and the new, massive commercial developments on Potsdamer Platz. The memorial should be a partner to them, not a private, quarantined space, cut off from the city. It should be vertical, highly visible and accessible to the thousands of people who participate in it by riding around it, walking through it or feeling it on the horizon. It is not only for the symbolic date but for the public at large; not for the relativity of private mourning, but an urban space of public awareness. So I did everything possible not to make it a private memorial by isolating it and cutting it off from the city or the country. Instead, I attempted to transgress the artificiality of the block structure which was drawn post-war, just very recently in fact, and to propose that the Memorial should continue to the Goethe statue in the Tiergarten, that it should open on both sides for people who are passing by in buses, cars, and on bicycles. It should be something which is visible and memorable in the light of Berlin. It should not stand as a didactic sign of a special relationship, but rather it should exist as an everyday event. After all, the Holocaust was an everyday event. It was not a special event; on the contrary, it was something that happened daily.

Do you believe such considerations are comprehensible for those moving within your models? Does one need some sort of reference work as a supplement to one's own intellectual efforts, in order to understand the multitude of references contained in your work? At least, wouldn't some sort of topographical view be helpful for understanding your concept for the Memorial?

I do not think it is good to try to make the Memorial into a set of signs which have to be deciphered,

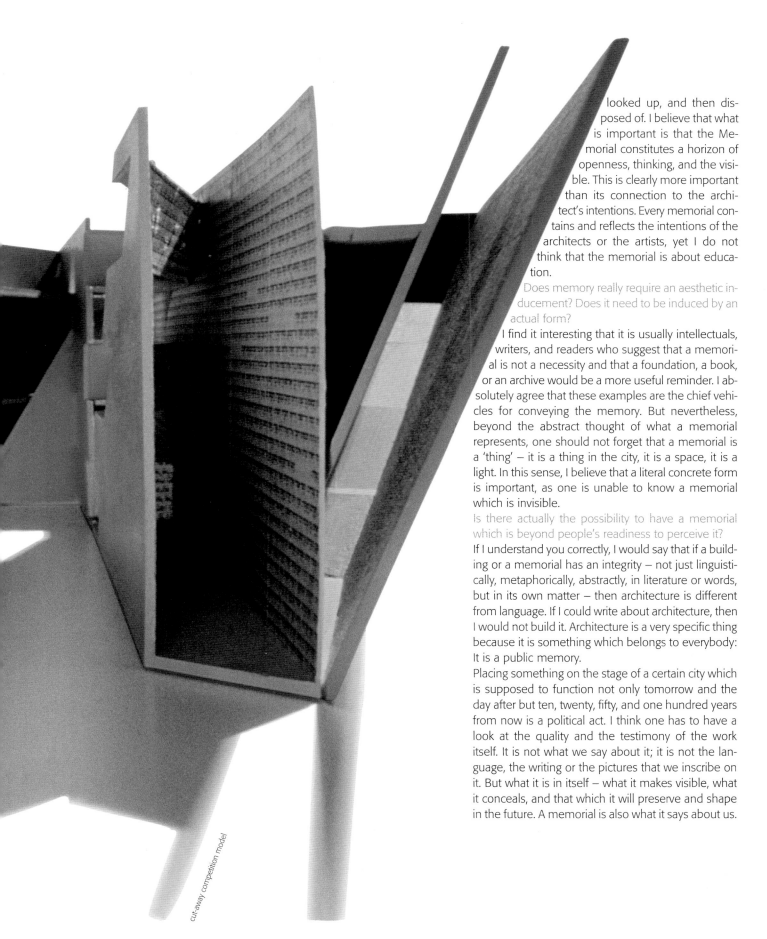

cut-away competition model

looked up, and then disposed of. I believe that what is important is that the Memorial constitutes a horizon of openness, thinking, and the visible. This is clearly more important than its connection to the architect's intentions. Every memorial contains and reflects the intentions of the architects or the artists, yet I do not think that the memorial is about education.

Does memory really require an aesthetic inducement? Does it need to be induced by an actual form?

I find it interesting that it is usually intellectuals, writers, and readers who suggest that a memorial is not a necessity and that a foundation, a book, or an archive would be a more useful reminder. I absolutely agree that these examples are the chief vehicles for conveying the memory. But nevertheless, beyond the abstract thought of what a memorial represents, one should not forget that a memorial is a 'thing' – it is a thing in the city, it is a space, it is a light. In this sense, I believe that a literal concrete form is important, as one is unable to know a memorial which is invisible.

Is there actually the possibility to have a memorial which is beyond people's readiness to perceive it?

If I understand you correctly, I would say that if a building or a memorial has an integrity – not just linguistically, metaphorically, abstractly, in literature or words, but in its own matter – then architecture is different from language. If I could write about architecture, then I would not build it. Architecture is a very specific thing because it is something which belongs to everybody: It is a public memory.

Placing something on the stage of a certain city which is supposed to function not only tomorrow and the day after but ten, twenty, fifty, and one hundred years from now is a political act. I think one has to have a look at the quality and the testimony of the work itself. It is not what we say about it; it is not the language, the writing or the pictures that we inscribe on it. But what it is in itself – what it makes visible, what it conceals, and that which it will preserve and shape in the future. A memorial is also what it says about us.

SPACE

When talking about the Jewish Museum, the term space comes up constantly. What does "space" mean to you?

Well, space is everything and nothing. On one hand, space represents the outer space. the Universe, yet we also have a notion of the inner space which is a kind of interiority. However, clearly the word space is not adequate when it comes to building. Building is simultaneously completely external, remaining outside, and imbued with a physiognomy which is also internal.

Thus, architecture presents a very radical view. It is very functional when dealing with hammering, knocking down, breaking, constructing, and making new things, and yet it is the deepest and the most far-reaching transformation of identity.

Space, as a word, can be used to cover everything from the most distant planets and the molecular structures inside the smallest structures in the universe to the space of the soul, which encloses … What does it enclose?

INSIDE AND OUTSIDE

These are dialectical, Hegelian notions, coming from the dialectic of the Greeks. They are very abstract forces, and not all cultures deal with these categories. If one looks, for example, in the Bible, in the Jewish tradition, one finds very little about ‚inside' and ‚outside' and very little about objects as opposed to their density in human experience.

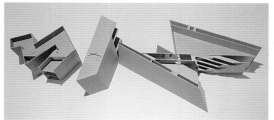

There is very little to reconstruct Noah's Ark and the Temple of Solomon, yet the Jesuits, in particular, have tried it for centuries, since these are constructs that were given by God himself. When one gets down to it, one realizes that the image is transformed by a different attitude to those concepts. In fact, even the language is different because of it.

I am not sure if I am really answering your question. However, I would say that one could leave these categories. One could be quite oblivious to the big dialectical forces – the categories of ‚inside and outside' and ‚space and time' – and simply deal more pragmatically and more empirically with such a thing as making a building, a house, an apartment block, or an office building. And I actually attempt to do this. I wonder what I would do to change such an unchangeable thing and to make it even one degree closer to the meridian of humanity.

After all, in Hebrew, the Deed, the Word, the Thing and the structure are one word, and that is the meaning of God's creation

No, I always thought the facade had … well, we know the history of it. We know how buildings became as thin as the people looking at them and so surface-like that the facade was born as a new aesthetic element of a reduced reality. I don't think it is the time of the facade anymore. It is a different time and while the word ‚facade' might still be around, I don't think anyone is looking at them, even if the architects of Berlin are still constructing them.

THE JEWISH CEMETRY IN WEISSENSEE, BERLIN

When I came to Berlin, I visited the cemetery, which was still in the eastern part of the city, and I was extremely shocked when I saw it. I had read about the Jewry of Berlin: how integrated and assimilated the Jews of this city were vis-à-vis the Jews of Poland and other countries who were not nearly as successfully integrated into society.

What struck me when I visited the cemetery was its emptiness. The tombstones were huge granite slabs, stretching for many meters long and high. There was no one left to visit. There was almost no evidence of Hebrew letters or symbols. And it was built, somehow, for the future of a community which hardly had any future. This phenomenon is truly poignant.

The emptiness that I witnessed at the cemetery actually confirmed my idea of the 'void' as an architectural device.

The 'voids' of the Museum provide a setting for nothing really to be displayed, because there is nothing really to be seen. It is just an emptiness which will never be eliminated from this city.

But the Weissensee cemetery, if anything, gives a historiographic reference for the confident and catastrophic assimilation as well as for the catastrophic misunderstanding of that community and

TRADITION AND THE NEW

When we looked at the Jewish Museum before from above, from an angel's perspective so to speak, you stated that it was "a completely normal building." You don't like the term "avant-garde." And elsewhere, you even described yourself as a traditionalist. Yet, on the other hand, architecture critics consider you a deconstructivist.

Being called an avant-garde deconstructivist architect is not a label that I like. I don't believe that I am doing something which goes against tradition. But one would have to begin a discussion about tradition: Is tradition an imitation? Is tradition the unconscious, habitual reinforcement of the not-knowing? Or is tradition the grasping of the ungraspable and passing it on, having had a lot to do with it? And what part of it is passed on?

Let's take something traditional like the right angle. You appear to have something against right angles.

I am not allergic to the right angle, but it is a product of a spiritual history. It can only function within that spiritual history, and when that spiritual history is no longer decisive, the right angle also changes. Perhaps yesterday's perfection is no longer "right" for us.

And it is no coincidence that in German and English and in many other languages right and wrong are also associated with one another – the right, the orthogonal, the vertical versus the horizontal, man versus woman, earth versus God, light versus darkness, and good versus evil. It would be easy if the categories were still valid, but so many things have changed. We no longer operate with the right angle in the sciences, economics, chemistry, or in our daily life. So, it seems that we should ask: What do we operate with? What are our geometries? What are our orientations?

And then I could see how it might be right that Le Corbusier wrote the poem to the right angle, his last poem in which he celebrated the enigma of a vanishing world. It is not a coincidence that the world which we see today – in the news, in photographs, and on television – does not really look like that. Its shadows, its light, and its appearance are different. And there you have it: It is not right anymore; it is not quite right, because it does not quite appear in that constellation, but in fragments, approximations, indeterminacies …

I do not discriminate against the right angle; there are some right angles in the building of the Jewish Museum. I use right angles, but the right angle is also a product of tectonics, building construction and land surveying. It originated in Egypt from the division of land – mine versus yours. That is the original geometry as we know it. The original geometry does not have anything to do with aesthetics. It is about whose land ends where. And if we were in a different state we would also have a different view of the original geometry and we would find ourselves in a completely different geometrical, social and economic world.

What you have just recapitulated and described applies not only to right angles, but to all kinds of lines.

The line is different, because it covers so many paradoxical phenomena. The lines of reality cannot be reduced to geometry. I've often talked about the line; well, architecture is full of lines. It is a discipline of lines, and it is also always in line with what is impossible. And very often it is a discipline with no point to the line. Additionally, the line often does generate the surface on which an activity could take place. And the line, one should remember, opens the non-linear field in which it is not the shortest distance between two points.

Two more key words relating to the architecture of the Jewish Museum: penetration and transparency.

There are different kinds of transparency and different kinds of penetration. Most people would take transparency as simply meaning what can be seen through, but glass is not necessarily the most transparent material.

I think your formulation of penetration and transparency is profound. Transparency has a different aura and is a different field of experience. That is why we can not see with the backs of our heads, after all, everybody has had that experience walking in a dark street at night.

Penetration is the projection of the project; the dynamic movement between the support and its surface: the explosive moment. Even walls can be seen through.

There is always the permanent problem of architecture: the linguistically definable area of experience does not necessarily coincide with architectural space. There is architecture which moves towards other experiences, experiences that have to do with human beings and which are not confined to verbiage.

OSSIETZKY'S CUP

I think that the beauty of architecture is in how one first experiences it from a distance, then how one comes close to it and can touch it. At this point, one can also do something with it kinetically in one's mind. I am very much interested in that spirit.

Certainly, the materials I used in Berlin are not the materials that I use in London or elsewhere in other projects, because, for me materials are like Ossietzky's cup which appears in a mysterious poem by Paul Celan. The poem is enigmatic. I have asked many literary experts to explain this Paul Celan poem to me. It refers to a tin cup, to the material, and the words themselves are like tin, even for someone like me, who doesn't read German as his mother-tongue.

So, there is a contamination between that which we understand and are unable to communicate, and that which is there with the things themselves and seems to resist even the language with which it could be manipulated.

That is, in my opinion, also a very interesting point about architecture: We can speak about it, we can interpret it, we can intellectually dissolve it, but in the space of the city it continues to play another role. Architecture plays a role which resists. Interestingly, it functions as a resistance to people , and yet is made by them. What a fascinating field! It is a field which originates through its speaking and through language, and yet it is something that is very often oblivious to what we can say about it. It is very often mute, not just silent.

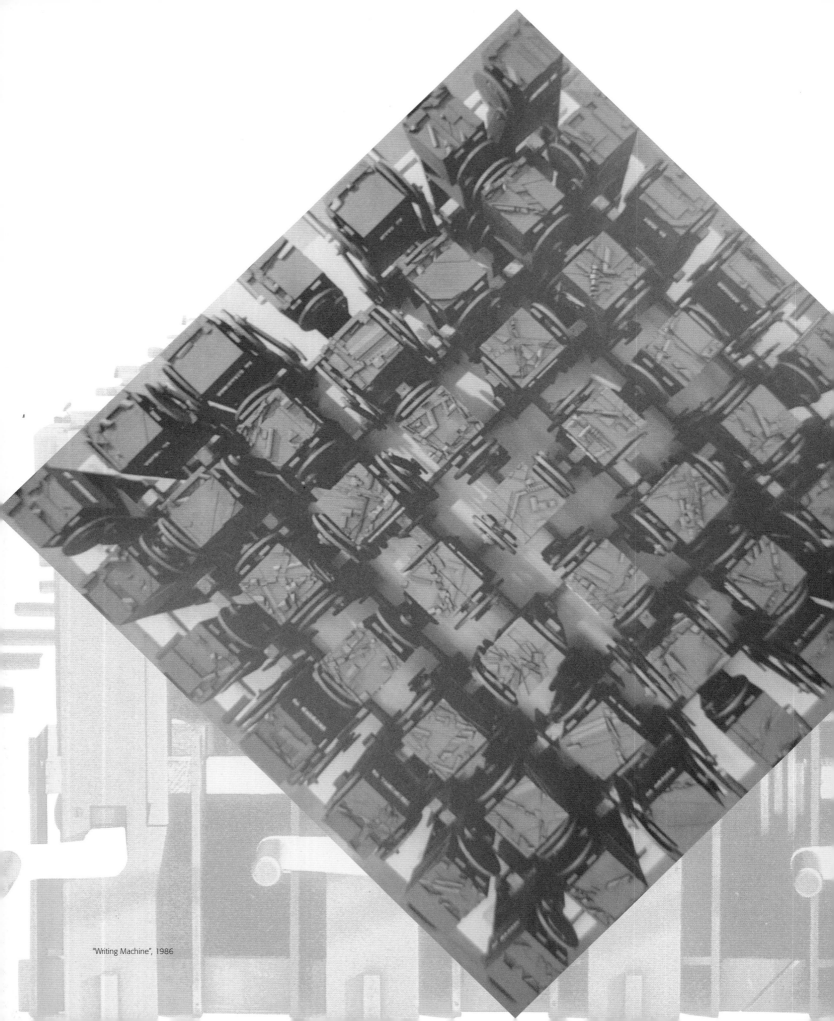

"Writing Machine", 1986

What meaning do the materials that you chose to use for the Jewish Museum have for you?
Materials alone are nothing. Only when they are placed into a certain context do they begin to have a human dimension. I use, for example, zinc in the building, not the new zinc which is pre-weathered and already stabilized, but the more traditional form of zinc, which will take some years to become part of the city. It will change; it will oxidize, it will become blue-gray; it will change its porosity depending on whether its orientation is north, south, east or west. I used it simply because I liked it.

I think it's the right color and the appropriate covering for such a large building with such a large facade. The building is steel and concrete, yet it is covered, because such a big structure should be softened for its presentation on the street. The building will not look like a shiny machine.

One already notices from street level that there are numerous incisions that have been placed on the exterior of the building, but that also seem to reach into the immaterial, into the sky. These are clearly not ordinary windows. And these windowless moments, these lines of light are repeated for the visitor inside the building, almost like the relationship between a negative and a positive.

The light which comes in and out of the Museum doesn't come through normal windows, as there are no conventional windows in the building. Of course, there are places where you can see the sky, where you can see the street, and where you can look across, but they have never been conceived as traditional windows, as holes in the walls, which are there to look out of. They were generated by a completely different logic of openness. It is not the openness of an elevation that an architect could plan. Nor is it the openness of a system of geometric compositions. Instead, it is the openness of what remains of those glimpses across the terrain – glimpses, views, and glances that are sometimes very accidental, yet are the disciplined longitude-latitude lines belonging to a projection of addresses traversing the addressee.

Walking through the E.T.A. Hoffmann garden, one can't help noticing that the floor is tilted. What role do the visitor's physical being and self-awareness play for you?

I think architecture begins simulaneously with the head and with the feet. One has to experience it seeing it from afar and by walking through it. Later on one might actually think about it, but I think one experiences it first with one's ankles and shoes. In my opinion, that is where it begins: It begins at the ground. The E. T. A. Hoffmann garden represents an attempt to completely disorient the visitor. It represents a shipwreck of history. One enters it and finds the experience somewhat disturbing. Yes, it is unstable; one feels a little bit sick walking through it. But it is accurate, because that is what perfect order feels like when you leave the history of Berlin.

It is the only orthogonal square form. It is the only perfectly right-angled form in the entire building which has both right-angles in plan and right-angles in section, and yet it is the one form which I think people will feel strangely alienated from after experiencing it. It feels a bit like sailing in a boat; it is like being at sea and discovering that everything suddenly seems very different. And doesn't Berlin look different from that exile, even for Berliners who never left the place? It is an upside down garden with the earth remote inside concrete columns, roots above, hard ground below, and vegetation intertwined above – out of reach.

DRAWING

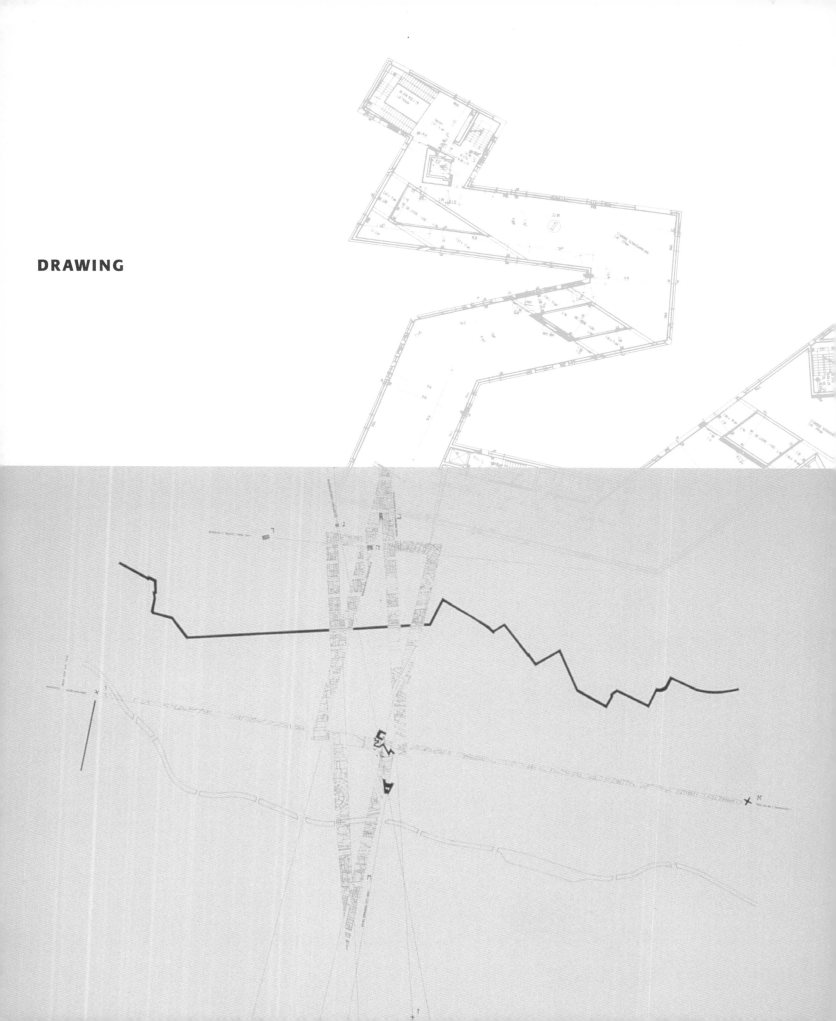

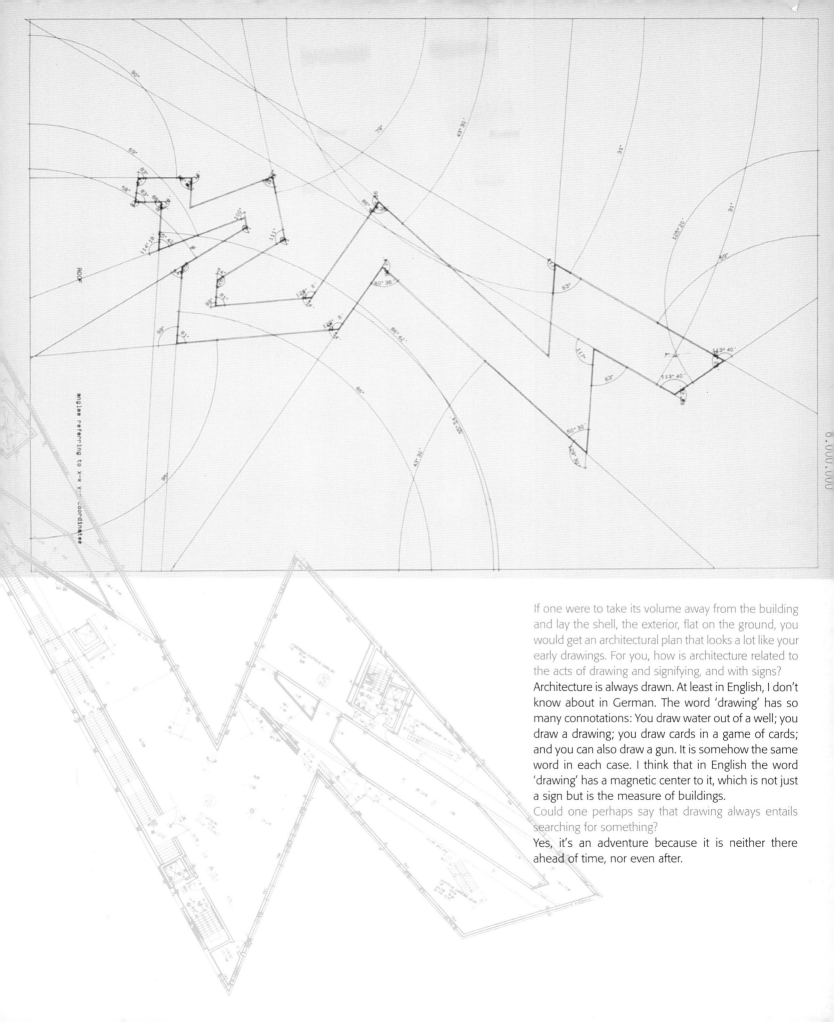

If one were to take its volume away from the building and lay the shell, the exterior, flat on the ground, you would get an architectural plan that looks a lot like your early drawings. For you, how is architecture related to the acts of drawing and signifying, and with signs?

Architecture is always drawn. At least in English, I don't know about in German. The word 'drawing' has so many connotations: You draw water out of a well; you draw a drawing; you draw cards in a game of cards; and you can also draw a gun. It is somehow the same word in each case. I think that in English the word 'drawing' has a magnetic center to it, which is not just a sign but is the measure of buildings.

Could one perhaps say that drawing always entails searching for something?

Yes, it's an adventure because it is neither there ahead of time, nor even after.

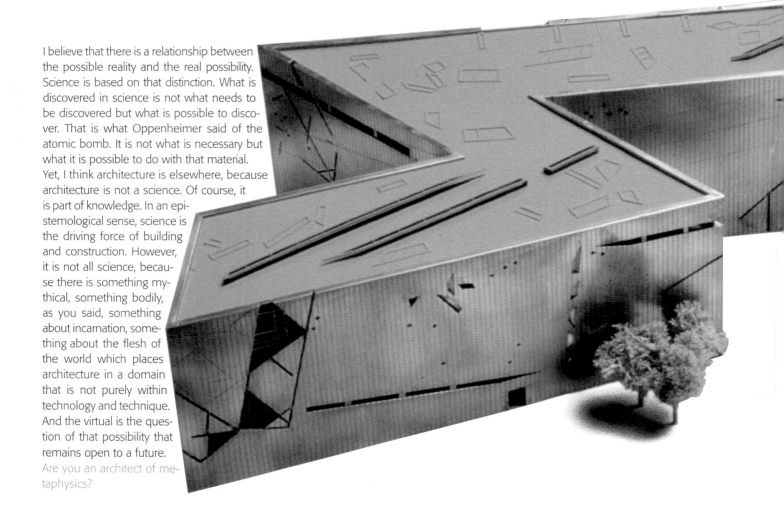

I believe that there is a relationship between the possible reality and the real possibility. Science is based on that distinction. What is discovered in science is not what needs to be discovered but what is possible to discover. That is what Oppenheimer said of the atomic bomb. It is not what is necessary but what it is possible to do with that material. Yet, I think architecture is elsewhere, because architecture is not a science. Of course, it is part of knowledge. In an epistemological sense, science is the driving force of building and construction. However, it is not all science, because there is something mythical, something bodily, as you said, something about incarnation, something about the flesh of the world which places architecture in a domain that is not purely within technology and technique. And the virtual is the question of that possibility that remains open to a future. Are you an architect of metaphysics?

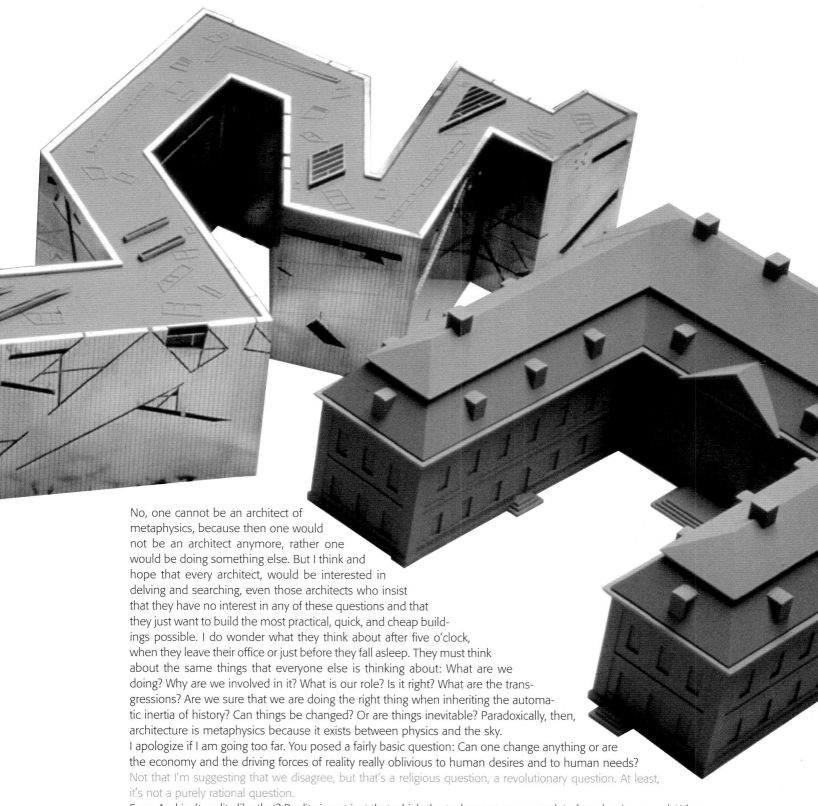

No, one cannot be an architect of
metaphysics, because then one would
not be an architect anymore, rather one
would be doing something else. But I think and
hope that every architect, would be interested in
delving and searching, even those architects who insist
that they have no interest in any of these questions and that
they just want to build the most practical, quick, and cheap buildings possible. I do wonder what they think about after five o'clock,
when they leave their office or just before they fall asleep. They must think
about the same things that everyone else is thinking about: What are we
doing? Why are we involved in it? What is our role? Is it right? What are the trans-
gressions? Are we sure that we are doing the right thing when inheriting the automa-
tic inertia of history? Can things be changed? Or are things inevitable? Paradoxically, then,
architecture is metaphysics because it exists between physics and the sky.
I apologize if I am going too far. You posed a fairly basic question: Can one change anything or are
the economy and the driving forces of reality really oblivious to human desires and to human needs?
Not that I'm suggesting that we disagree, but that's a religious question, a revolutionary question. At least,
it's not a purely rational question.
Sure. And isn't reality like that? Reality is not just that which the technocrat can control. In fact, that is not real. What
they can control cannot be real. To me the only real thing is that which cannot be controled. Look at the collapse of the
Soviet Empire right here in Berlin. Who would have ever predicted that such a powerful constellation of forces would be
nothing in comparison to human desire, to the thoughts of a few poets or writers who were imprisoned or killed, to the dreams
of Berliners.

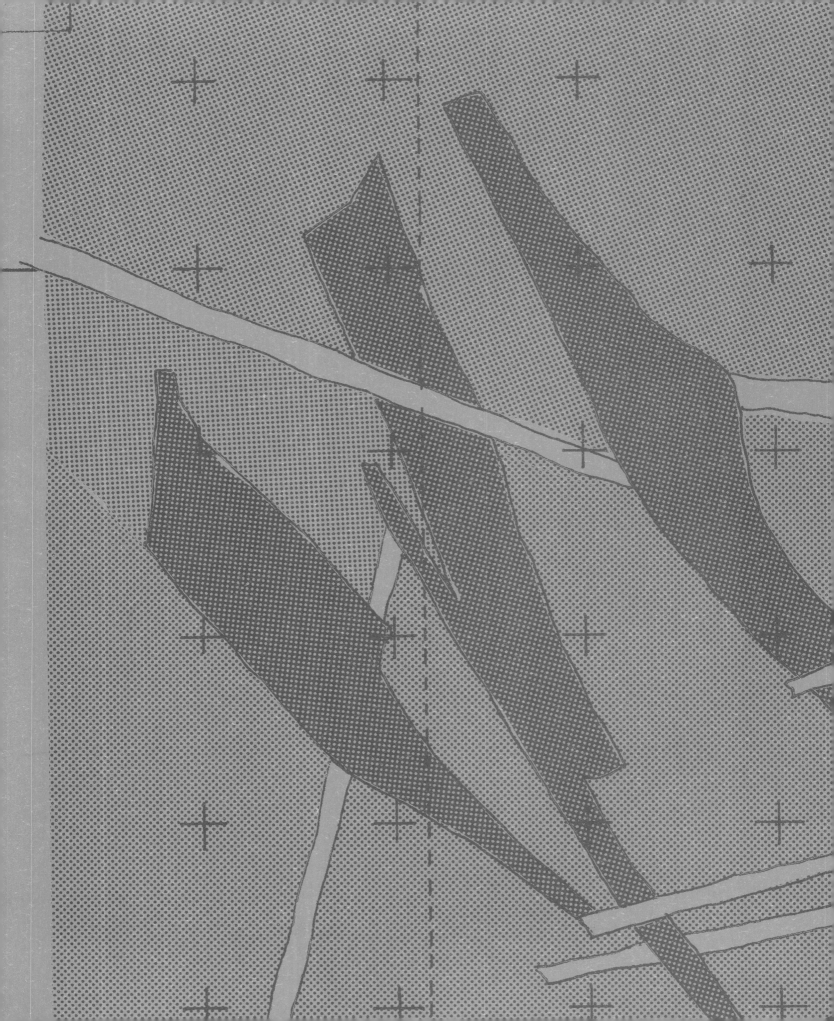

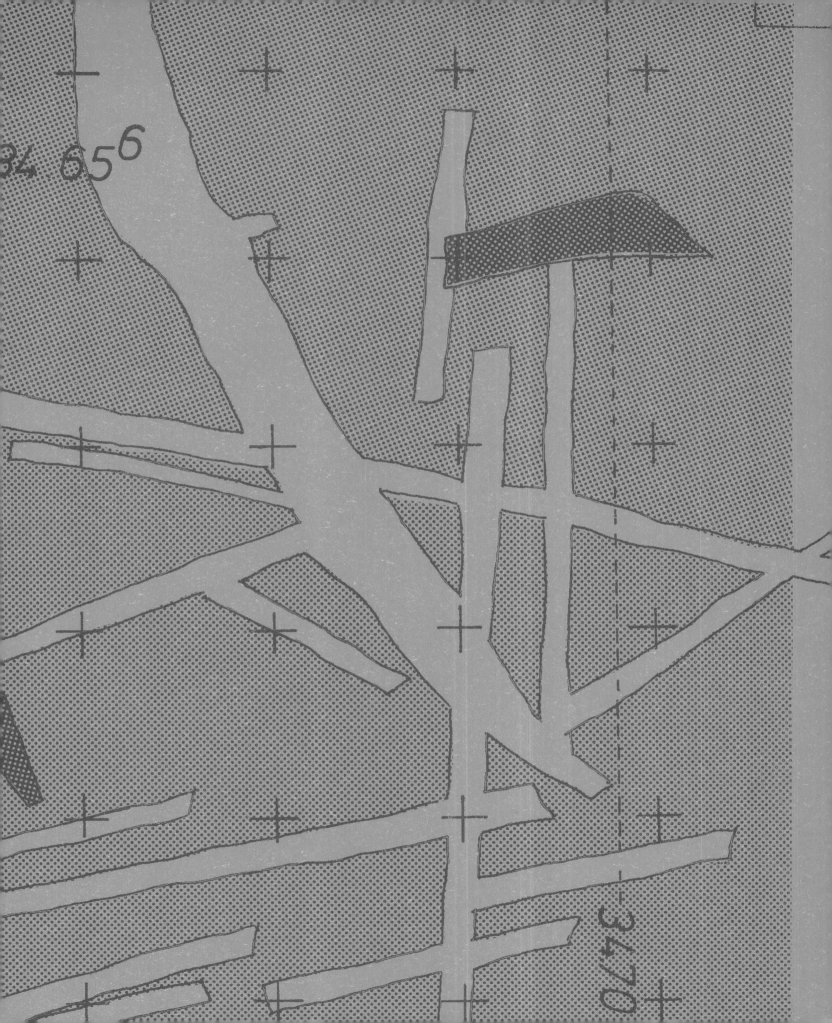

PHOTO ESSAY BY HÉLÈNE BINET

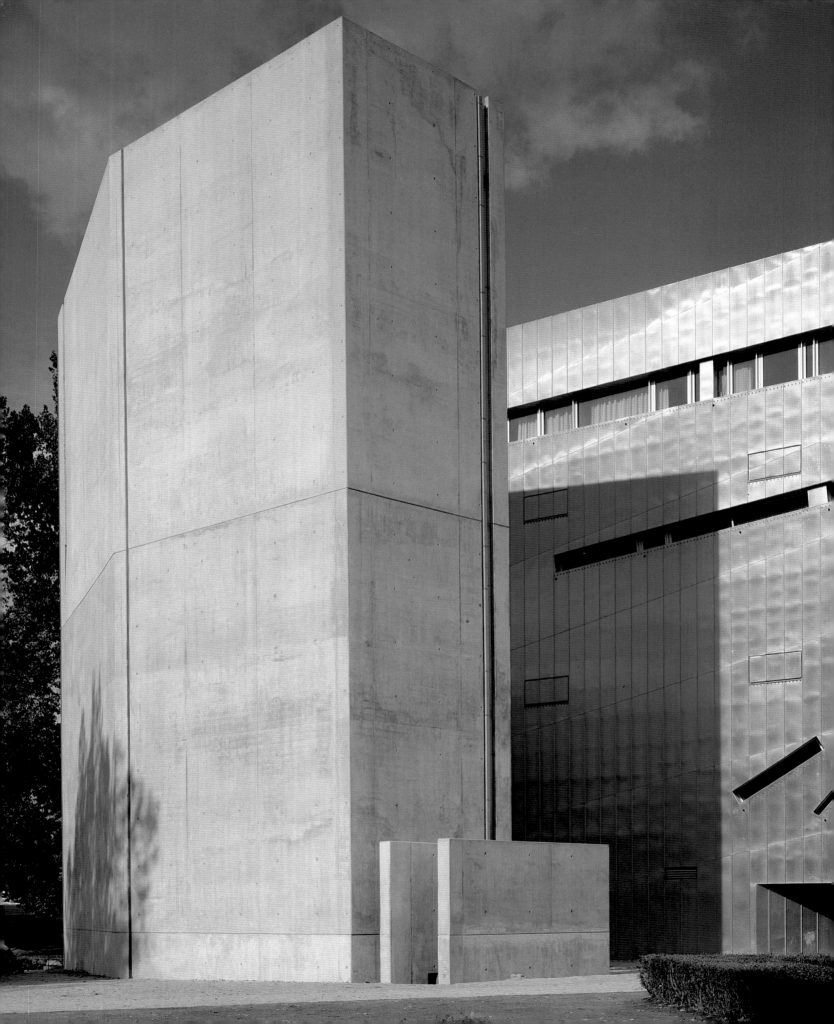

The E.T.A. Hoffmann garden represents an attempt to completely disorient the visitor. It represents a shipwreck of history. One enters it and finds the experience somewhat disturbing. Yes, it is unstable; one feels a little bit sick walking through it. But it is accurate, because that is what perfect order feels like when you leave the history of Berlin.

I use zinc in the building, not the new zinc which is pre-weathered and stabilized, but the more traditional form of zinc, which will take some years to become part of the city. It will change; it will oxidize; it will become blue-gray; it will change its porosity depending on wether its orientation is north, south, east or west. I used it simply because I liked it.

The light which comes in and out of the Museum doesn't come through normal windows, as there are no conventional windows in the building. Of course, there are places where you can see the sky, where you can see the street, and where you can look across, but they have never been conceived as traditional windows, as holes in the walls, which are there to look out of. They were generated by a completely different logic of openness. It is not the openness of an elevation that an architect could plan. Nor is it the openness of a system of geometric compositions. Instead, it is the openness of what remains of those glimpses across the terrain-glimpses, views, and glances that are sometimes very accidental, yet are the disciplined longitude-latitude lines belonging to a projection of addresses traversing the addressee.

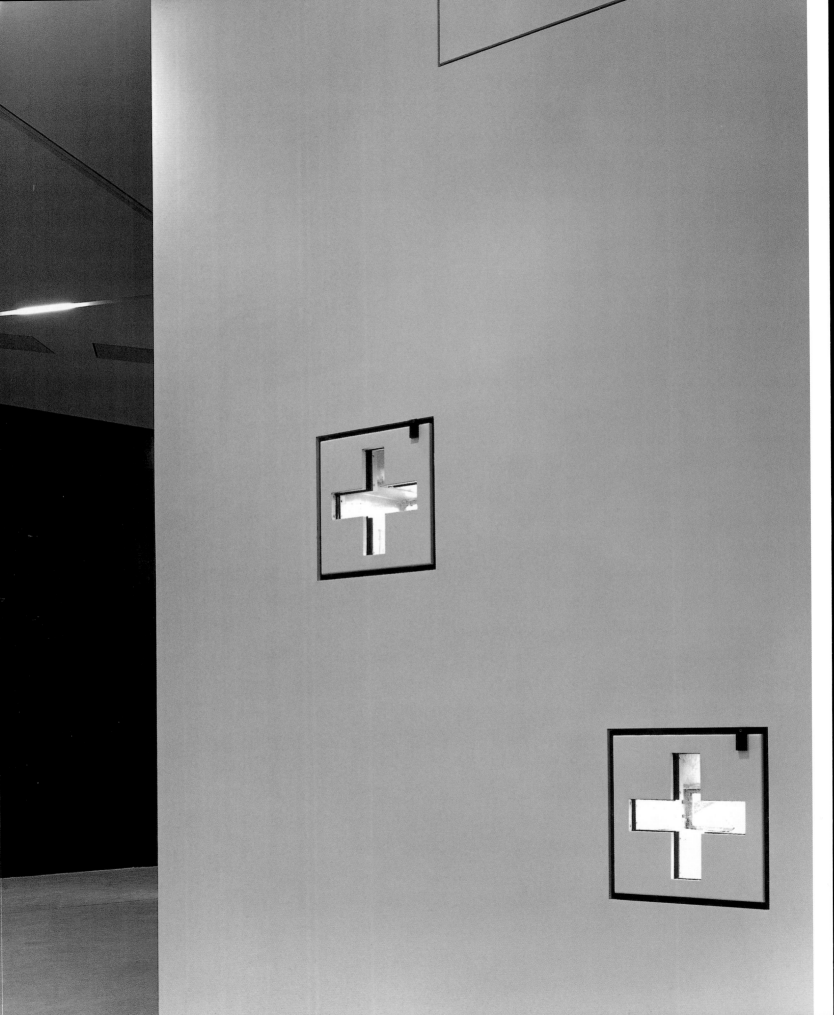

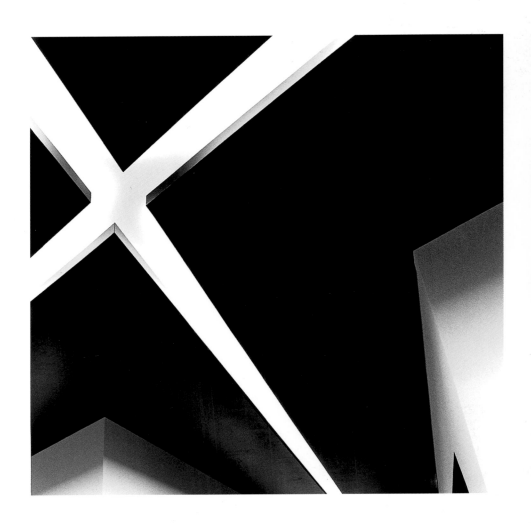

The "void" is a space you enter in the museum which organizes the museum, and yet it is really not part of the museum. I is not heated, it is not air-conditioned, furthermore it is not really a museum space. Yet "Die Leere" is something else which is very much a part of the space for an exhibition, – it is the space of Berlin, because it refers to that which can never be exhibited when it comes to the Jewish Berlin history. It has been reduced to ashes.

I realize that there are people who are skeptical about the relationship between objects and space in the Museum. But people are also skeptical about the history of Berlin. Those very people who never wanted to see that history find it extremely difficult to accept the Museum. They say: 'Mr. Libeskind, now it is very difficult to address this issue.' But yes, it is difficult, and that is why it is so very important to do so.

Berlin is also in exile from itself; that is to say, it is distant from itself and not reachable again along the same road. It is as if there is an access, or a street, leading to a dead end of the city which is all of us. Beyond that event, there is a completely different city. The city is apocalyptic, reborn out of something impossible. There is also the street of connections, which continues across all of these vulnerable cataclysms to contain the main connection named Berlin.

THE JEWISH MUSEUM IN BERLIN

Past – Present – Perspectives

Helmuth F. Braun

With the building by Daniel Libeskind, the Jewish Museum in Berlin becomes a venue well-suited for representing the history of the Jews in Germany in all its vicissitudes and preserving the material evidence of Jewish culture. After a prehistory that came to a tragic end on the night of the pogrom in 1938, after an over 20-year interim solution as the Jewish division of the Berlin Museum with exhibition spaces in the Martin-Gropius-Bau, and after a six-year construction period, the new museum – the subject of considerable controversy in the press as well as in architectural and museum circles – is now being opened to the public. With its zigzag form, silver metallic facade, irregular window slits, voids, and subterranean axes, with its exile garden and Holocaust memorial, the spectacular building forcefully marks the civilizational rupture that occurred in German history with the rise of National Socialism. For the Jewish community, for the Jews of Berlin and Germany, the museum is intended as a locus of identification and self-affirmation; for the majority of German visitors, it will serve as a place of education, encounter, and tolerance toward minorities. While the Jewish Museum seeks to open itself above all to the present and the future, the awareness of its tradition remains equally inescapable; thus here, too, it is appropriate to begin with a look back into the past.

Alexander David (1687–1765), a banker at the court of the duke of Braunschweig, was among the first collectors of Jewish ceremonial objects as art objects. After his death, his collection of aesthetically significant Jewish ceremonial objects was bequeathed to the Jewish congregation in Braunschweig.

The first private collection of Jewish ceremonial objects to attain public notoriety was that of Isaac Strauss (1806–1888), grandfather of the anthropologist Claude Levi-Strauss. Strauss's collection was shown to the public for the first time at the 1878 world exposition in Paris; the accompanying catalogue is now considered the earliest

documentation of an exhibition of Jewish ceremonial objects. This exhibition, intended to showcase the craftsmanship of French Jews, was innovative for its subordination of the ritual function of the objects to their formal and aesthetic qualities. Most of the objects, elaborately worked in precious metals, were numbered and catalogued by Strauss himself. In 1889, a donation by Nathalie de Rothschild enabled the Musée de Cluny, the most important museum of applied arts in France, to acquire the Strauss collection.

In 1887, less than a decade after the Paris exposition, an "Anglo-Jewish Historical Exhibition" was presented simultaneously in four different locations in London. With almost 3000 art and ceremonial objects, the sheer size and variety of the exhibition made it possible to classify the holdings and engage in meaningful stylistic analysis for the first time.

Without exception, the first Jewish museums in German-speaking Europe developed out of private collections of Jewish ceremonial objects. Shortly before the turn of the century, ethnological associations and small private museums began to be founded with the goal of preserving the material evidence of Jewish culture and making it accessible to Jewish and non-Jewish public alike.

The founding of the "Gesellschaft für Sammlung und Conservierung von Kunst und historischen Denkmälern des Judentums" ("Society for the Collection and Conservation of the Art and Historical Monuments of the Jews") in Vienna in 1894, the "Gesellschaft zur Erforschung jüdischer Kunstdenkmäler" ("Society for the Study of Jewish Art") in Düsseldorf in 1897, and the "Gesellschaft für jüdische Volkskunde" ("Society for Jewish Ethnography") in Hamburg in 1898 provided the institutional basis for the development of Jewish museums in German-speaking countries. These societies and associations were concerned not only with the local history of the Jews in the various cities in question, but with Jewish culture in general. Collections of "Palestinian antiquities," coins, manuscripts, and ceremonial objects were assembled, with different collections displaying differing emphases: the Hamburg collection, for example, focused on Jewish

above: **Silver Torah Shield**
Berlin, circa 1810
Silversmith: Carl Friedrich Hübener

above right: **Pair of Torah Finials**
(Rimonim)
Berlin, 1822–1852
Silver, partly gilded

below right: **Brass Chanukah Menorah**
circa 1925
Amstelveen, collection Willy Lindwer

ethnography, while that in Düsseldorf emphasized the artistic quality of Jewish cult objects.

The initiator of the Düsseldorf society was the art historian Heinrich Frauberger (1845–1920). Frauberger's efforts to build up a "collection of models," a library, an archive, and a collection of original Jewish ceremonial and art objects were ultimately aimed at the later establishment of a museum, whose holdings would be presented in special exhibitions and supplemented by loans from private persons and groups. Frauberger busied himself with the compilation of monument statistics, a topographical catalogue of Jewish art, and records of Jewish artists and their works. He produced numerous scholarly publications and established an information office where interested persons could learn about Jewish culture and congregations could obtain advice in matters such as the building of synagogues. Two years after his death, Frauberger's collection was acquired by the Jewish Museum in Frankfurt.

With their educational activities, these Jewish ethnographical associations and historical societies wished to encourage the preservation of material culture among the Jewish public. And to a certain extent, they succeeded: exhibition spaces were soon procured in Vienna, Frankfurt, and Hamburg, while many smaller Jewish communities established collections with local holdings. Not long afterward, Jewish art collections were shown to an interested public in Danzig (1903), Prague (1906), Warsaw (1910), and Berlin (1917). In 1906, Boris Schatz founded the Bezalel Art Institute and Museum in Jerusalem. Between 1912 and 1914, An-Sky (Salomon S. Rapoport), together with the "Jüdische, Historische, und Ethnographische Gesellschaft" ("Jewish, Historical, and Ethnographical Society") he had founded in 1908, studied, photogra-

Anonymous, **Yom Kippur at the Encampment of Metz**
after 1870
Cotton fabric, color print

Underground: **Shiviti Plate**
Poland 1925, (dated)
Indian ink, watercolor and zinc white on Paper

Julius Moser
Portrait of the Moritz Manheimer Family, 1850
Oil on canvas

Friedrich Georg Weitsch
Portrait of David Friedländer, ca. 1810
Oil on cardboard

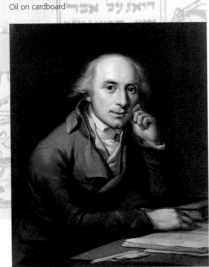

Anonymous
Portrait of Louis Lewandowski, 1868
Oil on canvas

phed, and documented the material culture of the Ashkenazim for an exhibition at the Jewish Museum in St. Petersburg in 1916. In 1920, the "Gesellschaft der Freunde jüdischer Antiquitäten" ("Society of the Friends of Jewish Antiquities") established a museum in Vilnius.

The first two decades of the 20th century were a high point in the history of Jewish museums in German-speaking Europe. Interest in the material evidence of their own history played an important role in the development of a new cultural identity among German Jews. Museum exhibitions served to present Jewish history and culture and lend visible expression to Jewish efforts for integration into German society.

In the 1920s, the problem of German-Jewish identity had become an integral element of museum work, with Jewish exhibition activities increasingly aimed at the non-Jewish public. This issue was also reflected in discussions of whether independent Jewish museums should be erected or whether Jewish divisions should be established within German museums. In 1927, Jakob Seifensieder donated a large collection of Jewish objects to the Germanisches Nationalmuseum. Later, such divisions were also established in Kassel, Mainz, and Braunschweig. Alfred Grotte of Breslau, on the other hand, called for the establishment of separate Jewish museums in the great centers of German Jewry.

In the history of Jewish museums, Berlin played a somewhat less prominent role. At the beginning of the 20th century, the Dresden jeweler Albert Wolf (1841–1907) began to assemble a private collection of Jewish cult objects. After his death, the collection was bequeathed to the Jewish congregation in Berlin and laid the foundation for the Jewish Museum there.

Jakob Steinhardt
Pharaoh's Destruction, 1911
Oil on canvas

right: Jakob Steinhardt
Hiob, 1913
Pastel on paper

In 1917, this "Kunstsammlung der Jüdischen Gemeinde zu Berlin" ("Art Collection of the Jewish Congregation in Berlin"), consisting primarily of coins, medals, synagogue textiles, ritual objects, and portraits, was presented to the public for the first time. In 1930, the art historian Karl Schwarz became director of the collection, which up to that point had been supervised by Moritz Stern, chief librarian of the congregation. Previously, Schwarz had founded a "Jüdischer Museumsverein" ("Jewish Museum Society"), intended to "awaken general interest in Jewish art and culture, and especially to further the art collection of the Jewish congregation of Berlin and develop it into a Jewish Museum." Unlike most Jewish museums, Karl Schwarz also collected works by contemporary Jewish artists. On January 24, 1933, only a week before the Nazis seized power, the Jewish Museum was inaugurated next to the synagogue on Oranienburger Strasse 31. Max Liebermann, chairman of the society, donated a self-portrait finished only a few days earlier. The painter Eugen Spiro expressed the hope that "in their esteem for the past, the congregation officials and Karl Schwarz would not forget the needs of living Jewish artists." In the entrance hall, next to busts of Moses Mendelssohn and Abraham Geiger, works by contemporary Jewish artists were programmatically displayed as well, including Arno Zadikow's sculpture "David" and Lesser Ury's biblical portraits of Jeremiah and Moses, as well as Jakob Steinhardt's great expressionist painting "The Prophet" from 1913.

In the summer of 1933, Karl Schwarz emigrated to Palestine, where he assumed leadership of the newly established municipal art museum at the request of Tel Aviv mayor Meir Dizengoff. Erna Stein-Blumenthal succeeded him at the museum in Berlin, until she too emigrated to Palestine in May of 1935. Under her aegis, a double exhibition with works by Eugen Spiro and Ludwig Meidner was shown in 1934, as well as a portrait exhibition. An exhibition on the doctor and philosopher of religion Moses Maimonides and a spring

Karl Schwarz
Director of the first Jewish Museum
in Berlin, 1933
Photograph

right: Lesser Ury
Moses on Mount Nebo
Pastel sketch on cardboard, 1927/28

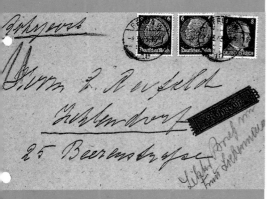

Letter from Martha Liebermann to Erich Alenfeld
sent by pneumatic tube on 4.3.43, 16.10 h (postmark)

Berlin, Pariser Platz 7

Thursday

Dear Mr. Alenfeld,

I am absolutely confused. The Bank hasn't even payed the small amount, without the friendly visit I would have remained without any money.
- At the same time everyone frightens me because of the deportation! I am eagerly awaiting you, after all Dr. Landsberger was supposed to come.
Please, please give me an answer.

Gratefully
yours
Martha L.

added by Erich Alenfeld:
deported 5. III. 43
in the morning!
Taken poison!

exhibition of Jewish artists followed in 1935. After Erna Stein-Blumenthal, Dr. Franz Landsberger assumed direction of the museum, which was still able to present a number of significant exhibitions before it was forced to close on November 10, 1938. In 1936, the museum showed a memorial exhibition on Max Liebermann and Max Fabian, the Reichsausstellung of Jewish artists, as well as a show entitled "Unsere Ahnen" ("Our Ancestors"). In 1937, exhibitions followed commemorating the 500th birthday of the great Jewish-Spanish scholar, biblical exegete, and statesman Don Jizchak Abrabanel, as well as the 100th anniversary of the death of Rabbi Akiba Eger, a Talmudic authority who lived and worked in the first half of the 19th century in Brandenburg-Friesland and Posen. Both exhibitions were organized by the art historian Rachel Wischnitzer-Bernstein. In the same year, the exhibitions "Das Jüdische Plakat" ("The Jewish Poster") with works by Ernst and Alexander Oppler and "Hundert Jahre jüdische Kunst aus Berliner Besitz" ("One Hundred Years of Jewish Art from Berlin Collections") were also shown. In 1938, under pressure of increasing persecution and exclusion, the museum presented its last show, an exhibition of ceremonial objects entitled "Aus kleinen jüdischen Gemeinden" ("From Small Jewish Congregations"). This small exhibition showed objects from Jewish congregations "that have been dissolved in recent years or whose worship spaces have been subject to restrictions, so that they are no longer able to properly care for their old, piously tended, and often valuable possessions." After the pogrom on Kristallnacht, the holdings of the museum were confiscated by the Nazis, and Franz Landsberger was arrested and taken to Sachsenhausen. After his release, he succeeded in emigrating to England and later to the United States.

The obliteration and dispersion of the great Jewish populations of central and eastern Europe and the destruction of the museums and private collections that had recorded their existence and paid tribute to their long, rich history left a cultural vacuum in its wake, a void that to some extent was filled by the newly founded museums in the United States and in Israel. In post-war Germany, Jewish concentration camp survivors and returning exiles concentrated their energies first and foremost on the reconstruction of a functional community and on achieving recognition for their claims to restitution and reparations by the Federal Republic of Germany; thus at first, no attention could be devoted to the establishment of a new Jewish Museum. Nor would any exhibition pieces have been available for such a museum: these had been confiscated by the Nazi authorities after 1938 and had disappeared or been destroyed or melted down in the course of the war.

A few months after the end of the war, a large portion of the painting collection of the former Jewish Museum was rediscovered in the cellar of the former Reichskulturkammer on Schlüterstrasse. The body of works was confiscated by the Allied restitution authorities for distribution to Jewish institutions. The majority of the works went to the Bezalel Museum, later the Israel Museum, in Jerusalem, with a small portion going to Hebrew Union College in Cincinnati. Today, only a few pieces from the former collection are once again in the possession of the Jewish community of Berlin, among them Jakob Steinhardt's "The Prophet" of 1913.

In 1962, after the Berlin Wall made the Märkisches Museum inaccessible to citizens of West Berlin, the Berlin Museum was founded in the western part of the divided city by a citizens' initiative under the leadership of Edwin Redslob. In 1969, the Berlin Museum took up residence in a reconstructed Baroque Kollegienhaus on Lindenstrasse, providing the inhabitants of Berlin with a place to relive the history of their city. Already in the early stages of collecting activity for the Berlin Museum, isolated objects relating to the history of the Jews in Berlin were integrated into the collection. The impetus behind these acquisitions was to establish a monument to the life and work of the Berlin Jews as well.

The first major exhibitions of Jewish art shown in post-war Germany focused primarily on religious aspects, with exhibitions such as "Synagoga" mounted in 1960–61 in Recklinghausen and Frankfurt, "Monumenta Judaica" of 1963 in Cologne, and "Historica Hebraica" of 1965 in the Jewish community center in Berlin. The exhibition "Leistung und Schicksal" ("Achievements and Fate") shown in 1971 in the Berlin Museum, on the other hand, emphasized historical and cultural-historical aspects. Initiated by the Jewish congregation to commemorate the 300th anniversary of its founding, the exhibition was devoted above all to the history of the congregation and to Jewish life before and after 1933, as well as to various Jewish personalities. The concern of the exhibition was "to illustrate the close connection between Berlin and its citizens of Jewish origin, in the hope that even after a painful caesura, the best times of shared life and work may be revived once more in Berlin." As Heinz Galinski, chair of the Jewish congregation, wrote in the exhibition catalogue, this first historic presentation of Jewish art and culture in Berlin since 1938 "tells of both the brilliant highs and agonizing lows of Jewish life in this city. The exhibition emphasized a new, mutual trust and, in view of the positive public response, elicited the desire for a permanent exhibition in a "Berlin Judaica" division within the Berlin Museum.

In the eyes of those in positions of leadership at the time, the historical experience of the exclusion of the Jews during the Nazi period made it absolutely necessary to integrate a Jewish division into the museum of municipal history, in order to counter their renewed marginalization from the outset. Out of these considerations grew the idea of an extension building for the Berlin Museum, which in addition to a Jewish division, a coin collection, and a theater division would also accommodate desperately needed storage and functional spaces.

The idea of once again erecting a Jewish Museum in Berlin was at first associated with the reconstruction of the Ephraim palace, a project that had been approved by the senate in early 1975, but for which funds could not at first be secured. The urban palace, originally located at the edge of the Nikolai district and remodeled from 1762 to 1766 for Veitel Heine Ephraim, court agent of Frederick II, had been torn down stone by stone in 1935 in the course of the expansion of the Mühlendamm sluice, and had been stored in what would later be the western part of the city. In November 1975, the "Gesellschaft für ein jüdisches Museum in Berlin e. V." ("Society for a Jewish Museum in Berlin") was founded. The goal of this promotional society was "to reconstruct the Ephraim

Medieval Gravestones from the Spandau Demetery
from the permanent Exhibition at Martin Gropius Bau
1986–1991

palace, formerly at the Molkenmarkt, on a plot adjacent to the Berlin Museum as a part of that museum." The society, whose membership included numerous former Berlin Jews, comprised 130 members by the end of 1978.

In the same year, the Berlin Museum mounted the first exhibition of new acquisitions for the future Jewish Museum. In 1979, Dr. Vera Bendt was appointed as curator for the Jewish division and the future Jewish Museum to supervise the care and study of the growing holdings.

The realization of the Ephraim palace, however, proved more difficult than expected. The reconstruction of the Baroque palace on the corner of Lindenstrasse and Markgrafenstrasse, i.e. far from its original site in the Nikolai district, elicited considerable controversy among historic preservationists and architects. Finally, the situation changed radically in 1981, when the East Berlin magistrate decided to reconstruct the Ephraim palace near its historic location in the course of the renovation of the Nikolai district for the 750-year anniversary celebration of the city. With the decision to transfer the facade portions stored in the western part of the city to the magistrate of East Berlin, the plans to reconstruct the palace across from the Berlin Museum were laid to rest once and for all.

Shortly thereafter, the Berlin Museum succeeded in acquiring the Judaica collection of the Münster cantor Zvi Sofer, who had died in 1980, for the future Jewish Museum. In so doing, the senate demonstrated its continued support for the idea of an extension building. As a bill passed in parliament expressed it, "since the former Jewish Museum Berlin was dissolved in the Nazi period, its reestablishment as a division of the cultural-historical Berlin Museum must also be considered a kind of restitution."

In 1982, the museum received its first major gift when John F. and Hertha Oppenheimer, former citizens of Berlin, donated documents related to the activity of the "Centralverein deutscher Staatsbürger jüdischen Glaubens" ("Central Society of German Citizens of Jewish Faith") and the publishing house "Philo-Verlag," a gift that laid the foundation for the archival work of the Jewish division throughout the following years. In accord with its motto "Selbstverteidigung im Licht der Öffentlichkeit" ("Self-Defense in the Public Eye"), the Centralverein, active from 1893 to 1938, sought above all to mobilize its members to defend themselves against anti-Semitism. Numerous writings and brochures were published to equip them with necessary information, as well as the monthly magazine "Im deutschen Reich" and, from 1922 on, a newspaper read by two-thirds of German Jews. In 1919, the "Philo-Verlag" was founded in support of the defensive and educational activities of

Emil Orlik
Portrait of Walther Rathenau
ca. 1920, Oil on canvas

Gold Pocket Watch
18th century, according to family tradition
a gift of Moses Mendelssohn to his son-in-law
Simon Veit

Herbert Sonnenfeld
Ludwig Meidner with Self-Portrait, 1934
Photograph

Anonymous, **Map of Jerusalem**
after J. B. Villalpando
17th century, etching on hand-made paper

the Centralverein; like all Jewish publishing houses, however, it was closed after the pogrom in November 1938.

In 1984, following a successful exhibition on synagogues in Berlin, the museum decided to use the lecture hall on its ground floor as a permanent exhibition space for the Jewish division, since an alternative solution for an extension building could not be immediately found.

The official transfer of the art objects and archival materials acquired by the Gesellschaft für ein Jüdisches Museum to the state of Berlin in May 1985 constituted a public demonstration of support for the efforts of the Senatsverwaltung für Wissenschaft, Forschung, und Kultur (Senate Administration for Science, Research, and Culture) to find a suitable location for the extension building of the Berlin Museum with its Jewish division.

Meanwhile, in November 1986, the Jewish division opened three additional exhibition spaces in the reconstructed Martin-Gropius-Bau. Until the end of 1991, the exhibition "Juden in Berlin. Dokumente, Bilder, Kunstwerke" ("Jews in Berlin. Documents, Images, Works of Art") presented the Jewish division of the Berlin Museum to the public for the first time in its entire range with ceremonial objects, portraits of Jewish personalities, objects related to Jewish history, and works by Jewish artists as well as documents, photos, and mementos from the large holdings of the archive.

In the years that followed, the idea of an extension building for the Berlin Museum into which the Jewish division would be spatially, administratively, and conceptually integrated was repeatedly confirmed by various official agencies. Accordingly, the so-called "integrative model" was developed by Rolf Bothe, director of the Berlin Museum, and Vera Bendt, director of the Jewish division. This model emphasized the role of Jewish life as an integral element in the history of the city, as well as the representation of the "distinct history of the Jews" in religion and ritual, customs, family, and community history.

In a series of discussions at the Aspen Institute in March 1988, these concepts were presented to an international committee of experts. A consensus was reached, "not to erect a separate Jewish Museum, but one that belongs to the Berlin Museum. Architecturally, it must be clearly recognizable as an independent part of the overall building and … an independent part of the entire museum." It was agreed that the new museum would be called "Berlin Museum – Jewish Museum," and that the word "division" would be avoided.

These hurdles having been overcome, the plot south of the Berlin Museum was chosen as the site for the extension building. A spatial program was developed and the budget approved by the senator for financial affairs. In context of the solemnities on November 9, 1988, the Berlin senate announced the commen-

Sukkoth, 10th copper plate
from: Paul Christian Kirchner,
Jewish Ceremony, Nürnberg, 1734

Felix Nußbaum
Loneliness, 1942
Oil on canvas

cement of a realization competition for the "Erweiterung Berlin Museum mit Abteiling Jüdisches Museum" ("Extension of the Berlin Museum with the Jewish Museum division").

From among the 165 entrants, the jury chose the design by Daniel Libeskind, whose multiple zigzagged building, resembling a broken star of David, developed "a spatial and kinetic concept of interpenetration, refraction, superimposition, and temporary division." For Heinz Galinski, chair of the Jewish congregation, the project made it possible "to connect the 'achievements and fate' of the Jewish citizens of this city with the history of Berlin in an inescapable way. In the future, no one will be able to visit the Jewish Museum without perceiving the history of Berlin, and no one will be able to visit the future Berlin Museum without experiencing the history of its Jewish citizens in past and present."

After the fall of the Berlin Wall and the reunification of the two parts of the city after 28 years of separation, some began to advocate putting a stop to the building plans, and instead using the Ephraim palace or the Centrum Judaicum at the Neue Synagoge on Oranienburger Strasse as the Jewish Museum. The financial difficulties of the senate and Berlin's attempt to host the Olympics endangered the realization of the project. A letter-writing campaign, organized by the museum together with the architect Daniel Libeskind in the summer of 1991, raised broad support from the international public for the construction of a Jewish Museum in Berlin and put pressure on the Jewish community and municipal officials to hold to their original plans. Finally, in the fall of 1991, on the occasion of the transfer of ten paintings from the holdings of the former Jewish Museum as a permanent loan from the Israel Museum to the Jewish Museum in the Berlin Museum, then mayor Eberhard Diepgen announced that the extension building would be realized after the design by the architect Daniel Libeskind.

After a further phase of planning, which reduced the cost as well as the sculptural character of the building, the cornerstone was laid in a ceremony on November 9, 1992, with construction itself beginning in

Interior of the Liberal Synagogue,
Fasanenstrasse 79–80,
Berlin-Charlottenburg,
Architect: Ehrenfried Hessel, 1912
Reproduction of a color drawing

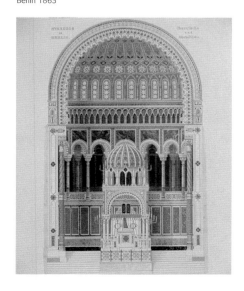

Friedrich August Stüler,
New Synagogue Oranienburger Straße ,
Sketch of the paintings for the east wall,
Lithograph
Berlin 1863

the following spring. In the course of construction, the Berlin Museum was closed and a total restoration of the Baroque building begun in October 1993.

Meanwhile, changes were occurring within the museum itself as well. In late 1992, long-time director Rolf Bothe moved to Weimar. At the same time, the two urban-historical museums, the Märkisches Museum and the Berlin Museum, began to take inventory of their collections with a view to establishing a single museum under the auspices of the foundation Stiftung Stadtmuseum. In the exhibition "Die andere Hälfte" ("The Other Half"), shown in November 1992 in the spaces of the Jewish Museum in the Martin-Gropius-Bau, a "representative selection of the artistic, documentary, and cultural legacy collected in the Märkisches Museum" was shown for the first time. These holdings, which complemented those of the

Jewish Museum, included documentation of the remains of the "Jewish silver" formerly held in the Märkisches Museum. These silver objects were confiscated from Berlin Jews in 1939 and acquired by Walter Stengel, then director of the Märkisches Museum, from the municipal pawnbroker for the price of the material. The holdings, placed in storage in 1943, were later lost and are now known only from the meticulous documentation.

In the summer of 1994, Amnon Barzel became the new director of the museum after his appointment by an international commission. Barzel made his explosive debut with the photographic exhibition "Überleben in Sarajevo" ("Surviving in Sarajevo") by the American photographer Edward Serotta, shown in the spring of 1995 in the shell of the new museum. In a brochure published for the topping-out ceremony in May 1995, Barzel made an initial statement of his concept for the Jewish Museum, a vision opposed to

Exhibition on the Architecture of Daniel Libeskind
in the Jewish Museum at Martin-Gropius-Bau
May 1994

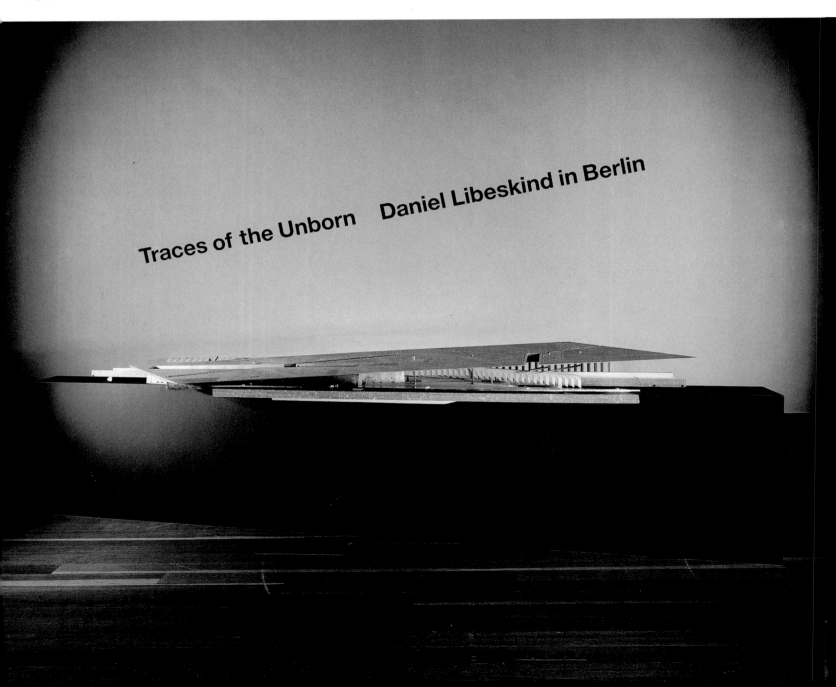

Traces of the Unborn   Daniel Libeskind in Berlin

Silver Chanukah Menorah
Berlin, circa 1776
Silversmith: George Wilhelm Marggraff

that of the city museum and the cultural senate. In a 50-page paper presented in October 1995, Barzel clarified his theoretical and practical ideas for cultural autonomy and his exhibition concept for the Libeskind building. In order to heal the dissent, the architect of the museum, Daniel Libeskind, was asked to mediate. In February 1996, a discussion group led by Libeskind with staff from both the Jewish Museum and the city museum presented a compromise concept, which, however, proved hardly feasible. The conflict, which increasingly shifted from the level of opposing concepts to the two main opponents themselves, was played out above all in the media, and in mid-1997 Amnon Barzel was dismissed from office. In late 1997, W. Michael Blumenthal was appointed as his successor.

During this period and until the closing of the Martin-Gropius-Bau in January 1998, three to four exhibitions a year were mounted by the Jewish Museum. These included an exhibition on architecture of the new Jewish school by Zvi Hecker, a presentation of the competition for the monument "Judenplatz Wien" in Vienna, a documentation on the exile in Shanghai, and finally an exhibition entitled "Erinnern heißt vergessen, was unsere Augen gesehen haben" ("To remember is to forget what our eyes have seen") in context of the major exhibition "Deutschlandbilder" ("Images of Germany"), with three artistic statements on the theme of memory by Penny Yassour, Minka Hauschild, and Joshua Neustein.

Since the time of the first presentations in the Berlin Museum and the establishment of the permanent exhibition in the Martin-Gropius-Bau, the collections of the Jewish Museum have continued to expand, above all with the support of the foundation Stiftung Deutsche Klassenlotterie Berlin. The museum possesses holdings that include ceremonial objects, with outstanding pieces by Berlin silversmiths and synagogue textiles from the 18th century; objects related to the history of the Jews, in Berlin and portraits of

View of the exhibit
Survival in Sarajewo
Photographs of Edward Serotta
in basement of construction site
April–June 1995

Jewish personalities including Giacomo Meyerbeer, Albert Einstein, Gerson Bleichröder, and Walther Rathenau; works by Jewish artists and representations of Jewish life with pieces by Max Liebermann, Ludwig Meidner, Lesser Ury, Jakob Steinhardt and Hermann Struck; a library with historic books and a collection of Jewish book art; and a historic archive with comprehensive collections of documents, photos, and memorabilia of personal and family histories from the 18th century to the present, among them numerous documents of individual fates during the Nazi period as well as life in exile.

Under the leadership of W. Michael Blumenthal, the Jewish Museum has finally attained the autonomy for which Blumenthal's predecessor fought in vain. The Libeskind building now houses an institution known as the "Jewish Museum Berlin." With its completion in late 1998/early 1999, the Jewish Museum will be distinct from the city museum and will be transferred to a separate foundation with its own personnel and budget. For a limited time, the Jewish Museum Berlin will be open for architectural tours. The museum itself — possibly the most important Jewish museum in Germany and perhaps even in Europe, with a large permanent exhibition on the history of German-speaking Jews and their relation to German history from earliest times to the present, temporary exhibitions on specific themes, a research and educational center, programs and lectures, extensive media facilities, an archive, and a library — is scheduled to open in the fall of 2000.

Berlin, November 1998

View of the exhibit
**Living in the Waiting-Room.
Exile in Shanghai** 1938–1947
Martin-Gropius-Bau, July/August 1997

Translation: Melissa Thorson Hause

Biographies

Daniel Libeskind

Born in postwar Poland in 1946, Libeskind became an American citizen in 1965. He studied music in Israel, (on the America-Israel Cultural Foundation Scholarship) and in New York, becoming a virtuoso performer. Leaving music to study architecture he received his professional architectural degree at the Cooper Union for the Advancement of Science and Art in 1970 in New York City and a postgraduate degree in History and Theory of Architecture at the School of Comparative Studies at Essex University in 1972.

Daniel Libeskind opened his architecture practice in Berlin in 1990 after winning the competition for the Berlin Museum with the Jewish Museum in 1989, which is open to the public since february 1999. His museum for the city of Osnabrueck, Germany, The Felix Nussbaum Haus, opened in July 1998.

Daniel Libeskind and his family now live and work in Berlin. He is registered as an architect in Germany with the Bund Deutscher Architekten (BDA). He is presently designing and constructing The Spiral Extension to the Victoria & Albert Museum, London; The Imperial War Museum – North, Manchester; the Bremen Philharmonic Hall, Bremen, Germany; The Jewish Museum in San Francisco, U.S.A; the JVC University – Colleges of Public Administration, Continuing Education and Art & Architecture, Guadalajara, Mexico; the Shoah Centre, Manchester, England; and the re-urbanisation plan for the former SS-lands in Sachsenhausen, Oranienburg.

Libeskind has taught and lectured at many universities worldwide. He was Head of the Department of Architecture at Cranbrook Academy of Art from 1978-1985 and subsequently founded and directed *Architecture Intermundium*, a private non-profit Institute for Architecture and Urbanism in Milan, Italy from 1986 to 1989. He was appointed a Senior Scholar to the John Paul Getty Centre; the Royal Danish Academy of Art; the Louis Sullivan Professor at Chicago; the Bannister Fletcher Professor at the University of London; the Davenport Chair at Yale University; member of the Akademie der Kunst since 1990; member of the European Academy of Arts and Letters and was among other universities a Guest Professor at Harvard University. Currently he is a Professor at UCLA and the Hochschule für Gestaltung, Karlsruhe, Germany.

Libeskind has been the recipient of numerous awards, most recently the American Academy of Arts and Letters Award for Architecture, the Berlin Cultural Prize and in 1997, he was awarded an Honorary Doctorate from Humboldt Universität Berlin as well as an Honorary Doctorate from the College of Arts and Humanities, Essex University. His work has been exhibited extensively in major museums and galleries around the world and also has been the subject of numerous international publications in many languages. His ideas have influenced a new generation of architects and those interested in the future development of cities and culture.

Selected Monographs:

Between Zero and Infinity, New York, Rizzoli, 1981.
Chamberworks, Architectural Association, London, 1983.
Theatrum Mundi, Architectural Association, London, 1985.
Line of Fire, Milan, Electra, 1988.
Marking the City Boundaries, Groningen, The Netherlands, 1990.
Daniel Libeskind, Countersign, Academy Editions, London, and Rizzoli Editions, New York, 1992.
Jewish Museum, Ernst & Sohn, Berlin, 1992, (winner of the book design award from the German publisher's commission).
Radix:Matrix:Works and Writings of Daniel Libeskind, published in German, 1994 and in English, 1997 by Prestel Verlag.
Daniel Libeskind: Kein Ort an seiner Stelle, Verlag der Kunst, Dresden, Germany, 1995.
El Croquis, published in Spanish and English, Madrid, Spain, November 1996.
Unfolding, Daniel Libeskind and Cecil Balmond, NAI Uitgevers/Publishers, Rotterdam, 1997.
Fishing from the Pavement, NAI Uitgevers/Publishers, Rotterdam, 1997.
Museum ohne Ausgang: Das Felix-Nussbaum-Haus des Kulturgeschichtlichen Museums Osnabrück – Daniel Libeskind, Dr. Thorsten Rodiek, Wasmuth Verlag, Tübingen, Autumn 1998.
Universale di architettura. Daniel Libeskind, Museo ebraico, Berlino. Text by Livio Sacchi, Testo & Immagine s.r.l., Torino. September 1998.

Selected Architectural and Urban Projects

Felix Nussbaum Museum, Osnabrück, Germany. Opened to the public July 1998.
The Jewish Museum, Berlin, Germany. Handover December 1998.
Jewish Museum San Francisco, San Francisco. Design Development. Begin construction 2000. Completion 2002.
The Spiral: Extension to the Victoria and Albert Museum, London, England. Competition. First prize, 1996. Design development. Awarded planning permission. Completion 2003.
Imperial War Museum – North, Manchester, Trafford, England. Competition. First prize, 1997. Design development. Completion date 2002.
Shoah Centre, Manchester, Trafford, England. Design development. Completion date 2002.
JVC University, Schools of Architecture, Teacher Training and School of Public Policy, Guadalajara, Mexico. Design development. Completion date 2001.

Uozu Mountain Pavilion, Uozu, Japan. Permanent landscape building and walkway for the seaside resort. Opened November 1997.

Polderland Garden, Almere, Netherlands. A steel garden for the city. Opened June 1997.

Bremen Philharmonic Hall, Bremen, Germany. Competition. First prize, 1995. Awaiting funding.

Sachsenhausen, Oranienburg, Germany. Urban design project for the former SS-lands. Special prize, 1993. City contract for B-Plan development, 1996.

Lichterfelde Süd, Berlin, Germany. Master plan accepted, 1994. Competition for housing estate, September 1997. Second prize including project to build. 1998.

Landsberger Allee, Berlin, Germany. Invited urban design competition. First prize, 1995.

Alexanderplatz, Berlin, Germany. Urban design competition. Second prize, 1993.

Potsdamerplatz, Berlin, Germany. Urban design competition, 1991.

Extension to the National Gallery, Dublin, Ireland. Competition Second prize. 1996.

New Synagogue and Jewish Community Center, Duisburg, Germany. Competition, Second prize. 1996.

New Ministry of Foreign Affairs, Berlin, Germany. Competition, 1996. Honourable mention.

Marking the City Boundaries, Groningen, Netherlands. Urban design and individual construction. 1994.

Wiesbaden Office Complex, Wiesbaden, Germany. First prize, 1992. To be realised.

Center for Contemporary Arts, Tours, France. Second phase. 1993.

Garden Pavillion, International Gardens Exposition, Osaka, Japan, 1990.

City Edge, Berlin, Germany. International Bauaustellung (I.B.A.) competition. First prize, 1987.

Daniel Libeskind: Beyond the Wall 26.36°, Netherlands Architecture Institute, Rotterdam. September 1997. Installation and concept for biographical exhibition.

Moscow-Berlin / Berlin-Moscow, 1900–1950 Exhibition, Martin-Gropius-Bau, Berlin, Installation and exhibition concept. 1995-96. First prize for Best Exhibition by the German Museum Directors Association.

George Grosz Retrospective Exhibition, Neue Nationalgalerie, Berlin / Staatsgalerie, Stuttgart,. Installation and Exhibition design for graphic works collection. 1994/95. Second prize for Best Exhibition by the German Art Critics Association.

"The Architect", Oslo National Theatret, Oslo. August 1997. Scenography and costume design.

"Metamorphosis", Gladsaxe theater, Copenhagen, Denmark. Scenography and costume design. 1994/95.

Hélène Binet

was born in 1959 in Switzerland, is a French architectural photographer based in London.

After studying in Rome, where she grew up, she worked for two years as a photographer at the Grand Theatre de Geneve before turning to architectural photography. Since then she has been working on a regular basis not only with Daniel Libeskind, but with Zaha Hadid, John Hejduk, Rem Koolhaas, Ben van Berkel, Coop Himmelb(l)au, David Chipperfield, Peter Zumthor and others.

Her work has been widely published in several architecure magazines and catalogues all over the world. Some of them are:
- *Peter Zumthor. Works. Buildings and Projects 1979–1997*, Baden 1998.
- *A Passage through Silence and Light*. Daniel Libeskind's Jewish Museum in Berlin, London 1997.
- The Museum Hamburger Bahnhof, Cologne 1997

In addition to this she works on regular basis for diverse publications as *AD, Archis, Blueprint, Daidalos* or *Domus*. Her works are regularly shown in solo exhibitions.

Helmut F. Braun

was born 1949 in Kirchseeon (Bavaria), studied literature, Sinology and Philosophy in Munich and Berlin. Since 1984, freelance assistant at the Jewish Department of the Berlin Museum. Since the 1989 architectural competition for the Berlin Museum, responsible for the project "Extension of the Berlin Museum with the Jewish Museum Department" until the final construction in 1999. Since 1995, curator at the Jewish Museum.